CREATIVE ENTANGLEMENTS

ROBERT S. DOMBROSKI

Creative Entanglements: Gadda and the Baroque

UNIVERSITY OF TORONTO PRESS
Toronto Buffalo London

© University of Toronto Press Incorporated 1999
Toronto Buffalo London

Printed in Canada

ISBN 0-8020-4490-5

Printed on acid-free paper

Toronto Italian Studies

Canadian Cataloguing in Publication Data

Dombroski, Robert S.
  Creative entanglements : Gadda and the baroque

  (Toronto Italian studies)
  Includes bibliographical references and index.
  ISBN 0-8020-4490-5

  1. Gadda, Carlo Emilio, 1893–1973 – Criticism and interpretation.
  I. Title. II. Series.

  PQ4817.A33Z635 1999   853'.912   C99-930366-x

This book has been published with the help of a grant from the City
University of New York.

University of Toronto Press acknowledges the financial assistance to its
publishing program of the Canada Council for the Arts and the Ontario Arts
Council.

In memory of Gian Paolo Biasin and
Gregory Lucente, *insigni gaddisti*

Contents

PREFACE ix

1 Gadda and the Baroque 3

2 Baroque Solitude: Disillusion and the Ruins of War 20

3 Creative Bodies: Theory and Practice of the Grotesque 43

4 A Baroque Ethics 74

5 A Baroque Mystery 96

APPENDIX: Gadda and Fascism 117
NOTES 135
REFERENCES 145
INDEX 149

Preface

In this book I have attempted to establish a definitive point of entry into the work of Italy's most original, intricate, and now most celebrated, contemporary Italian novelist, Carlo Emilio Gadda.[1] My foremost concern is to show how his aesthetic principles generate forms embodying a destructive power designed to combat the outrages of modern existence: namely, the conflictual life of risk and hazard generally associated with capitalist modernization. Among the many approaches to Gadda's world, the 'baroque' has seemed to me the most direct and useful. All of Gadda's texts incorporate strategies of deception and complexity; they combine elements of high and low culture in a way aimed at arousing the senses and provoking the mind, and the comic and lyrical drive behind them emerges from a melancholy oriented towards ruin and death. These are all essential features of the baroque.[2]

Gadda's baroque imagination also suggests a link with the main intellectual concerns of the present, as, for example, with the principles of cosmogenesis at the base of some of today's most challenging architectural theory. The cosmogenic world view, to quote Charles Jenks, 'is the idea that the universe is a single, unfolding self-organizing event, something more like an animal than a machine, something radically interconnected and creative, an entity that jumps suddenly to higher levels of organization and delights us as it does so' (Jencks 1995: 125).[3] According to this view, to understand the real as a system, we must be willing to abandon the Aristotelian–Christian conception of a rational external world in all of its mechanistic, modern variants in favour of a world that is in essence creative, unpredictable, and mysterious; a world not of linear design, but of twists, folds, undulations, and fractured planes; a world in which the unexpected and multivalent has supplanted the predictable and repetitive. The 'baroque' that Gadda sees in nature and that, he claims, he reproduces in his texts is such a world. To put it somewhat differently, in Gadda the search for depth is one with the need to delve into the complexity of the real, to examine the articulations of the most minute of fragments with a kind of dynamic, explorative play that transforms analysis into a wholly creative act.

The introductory chapter of this study has appeared in *Carlo Emilio Gadda: Contemporary Perspectives* (1997); chapter 3, in the volume *Studies for Dante: Essays in Honor of Dante Della Terza*, ed. Franco Fido, Rena A. Syska-Lamparska, and Pamela D. Stewart (1998). The appendix, 'Gadda and Fascism,' was originally published in Italian (Dombroski 1984). Here it appears translated and slightly revised in view of more recent discussions.

Quotations, with the exception of passages from letters and interviews, have been taken from *Opere di Carlo Emilio Gadda* (1988, 1989, 1991, 1992, 1993), published under the general editorship of Dante Isella. For *La cognizione del dolore* I have used William Weaver's English translation (*Acquainted with Grief* [1969]), while for *Quer pasticciaccio brutto de via Merulana*, I have used a combination of Weaver's *That Awful Mess on Via Merulana* (1985) and Robert De Lucca's as yet unpublished new English version of the novel, to which I have made slight amendations. All other translations from Gadda's works and criticism are mine, unless otherwise noted.

Acknowledgments

This book has benefited from the work of many colleagues and friends whose ideas I can only hope to have represented and recounted adequately. A special note of thanks goes to the readers of the University of Toronto Press for their kind words and valuable suggestions; to my editor at the Press, Ron Schoeffel, for all the support he has given to my Gadda projects; and to all my friends down on the farm, particularly Lucy Stone McNeece, my wife and most demanding critic.

ASHFORD, CONNECTICUT
OCTOBER 1998

CREATIVE ENTANGLEMENTS

1

Gadda and the Baroque

An obsession with knots; a penchant for extravagant verbal chemistry and intricate style; a desire to distort and pervert; a philosophical intelligence that seeks out obscure correspondences; a fascination with labyrinthine narrative structures, fragmentation, unpredictability, and obscurity – these are the characteristic features of Gadda's art that, from early on in his literary career, earned him the classification 'baroque,' a designation he vigorously defended against all pejorative associations, not the least being false and grotesque pedantry and, what amounts to the same, an excessive concern for artifice and ingeniousness. Gadda's defence of style, which serves both to ward off potential detractors and to set himself apart from his contemporaries, takes three intersecting tacks. The baroque (equated with the macaronic) is Gadda's weapon against all that in life and in literature is counterfeit, artificial, and spurious: against the hollowness of 'la retorica dei buoni sentimenti' (the rhetoric of noble feelings) and 'le parole della frode'[1] (the language of fraud). It is also his means of avenging what he calls repeatedly a cruel destiny of unspeakable hardships.[2] And, most important for this discussion, he sees the baroque as a quality of external reality; it exists in things, in history, and in nature.

Of the arguments Gadda employs in defence of his baroque manner, the most developed is contained in the imaginary dialogue with his editor ('L'editore chiede venia del recupero chiamando in causa l'Autore') that prefaces the first Einaudi edition of *La cognizione del dolore* (1963). Faced with the spectacle of lies, deceptions, and disorder of a diseased society (another commonplace of the historical baroque), the writer, Gadda argues, is stirred to derision which occasionally takes on hysterical proportions. His polemics, mockery, intolerance, general cruelty, and misanthropy, his 'baroqueness' and 'grotesqueness,' are all affected by the radically contradictory and uncertain reality in which the life of the subject unfolds. Thus if Gadda is 'baroque,' he is not so on account of a love for artifice and ornament, but because the world itself is baroque; for a writer, the task is to represent the reality of its baroqueness:

Il barocco e il grottesco albergano già nelle cose, nelle singole trovate di una fenomenologia a noi esterna: nelle stesse espressioni del costume, nella nozione accettata 'comunemente' dai pochi o dai molti: e nelle lettere umane o disumane che siano: grottesco e barocco non ascrivibili a una premeditata volontà o tendenza espressiva dell'autore, ma legati alla natura e alla storia [...]; talché il grido-parola d'ordine 'barocco è il G.!' potrebbe commutarsi nel più ragionevole e più pacato asserto 'barocco è il mondo, e il G. ne ha percepito e ritratto la baroccaggine'.[3]

[The baroque and the grotesque exist already in things, in the individual discoveries of a phenomenology external to us: in our very customs, in the 'common' sense of the few or the many: and in letters, be they humane or inhumane. Baroque and grotesque are not attributable to the author's premeditation or expressive propensities, rather they are linked to nature and history ...; so much so that the rallying call 'G. is baroque!' could be expressed in the more reasonable and serene assertion 'The world is baroque, and G. has perceived and depicted its baroqueness.']

And to those scholars who view the baroque as a category of the spirit or historical constant (Croce and Eugenio d'Ors, for example), Gadda remarks that

La natura e la storia, percepite come un succedersi di tentativi di ricerca, di conati, di ritrovati, d'un' Arte e o d'un Pensiero che trascendono le attuali nostre possibilità operative, o conoscitive, avviene faccino a lor volta un passo falso, o più passi falsi: che nei loro conati, vale a dire nella ricerca e nell'euresi, abbino a incontrare la sosta o la deviazione 'provvisoria' del barocco, magari del grottesco. (CD,761)

[Nature and History are perceived as the continual inquiry (attempts, corrections, and reformulation) of an Art or Mind that transcends our current operative and cognitive faculties, at times falling into error or errors. In the effort to understand, namely, through the investigatory or heuristic process, one encounters the baroque, even the grotesque, an obstacle or 'momentary' detour.]

Gadda goes on to say that the question of the relation between order ('Arte e Pensiero') and disorder ('the baroque and the grotesque') is internal and reciprocal. The baroque (disorder, disharmony, deformation, etc.) is therefore not the opposite of order, but a deep structure within a complex system. Confronted with this 'universal reality,' the subject of knowledge and discovery is caught in the labyrinth ('intrappolatosi in reiterate impasses'), and once he appears with great difficulty to have found an exit ('divincolatosi poi a mala esperienza esperita'), he becomes entangled again, and once again he attempts to free himself ('se ne sbroglia del tutto e di nuovo tende la via libera'); so he moves along a pathway towards 'la infinita, nel tempo e nel numero, suddivisione-specializzazione-obiettivazione del molteplice' (ibid)(the infinite, in time and number, subdivision-specialization-objectification of multiple realities).

What may appear here as random speculation are propositions constituting a philosophical position, developed early on, in the *Meditazione milanese*, into a cognitive mode that justifies a particular kind of *affect* or emotional reaction to the world, disclosed even in Gadda's earliest fictions and in the manifest anxieties of the *Giornale di guerra e di prigionia*. The self-reflexivity, parody, distortion, and infinite entanglements and references that characterize all of Gadda's texts, their excesses and instabilities, as well as their tendency to break down or dissipate in repetition, are at once symptoms and procedures, designed to distance and differentiate the writing subject from the national (and popular) cultural activity of his time. In certain respects, Gadda's writings (criticism and essays included) embody what, in a perceptive study of the Spanish literary baroque, has been called an 'aristocratic fetish of a highly wrought art form' (Beverley 1993: 59). The comparison is, of course, by way of analogy and could be extended to other forms of literary modernism (D'Annunzio, for example). In Gadda's case, we are obviously not dealing exactly with the same kind of ideological practice that characterizes the different forms of the historical baroque.[4] Yet, there is little doubt that Gadda's texts – as opposed to *prosa d'arte* and neorealism – are intended to escape the understanding of the masses and that they place themselves in stark opposition to popular bourgeois cultural practices by virtue of the uniqueness of the writer's biography and experience, which accounts for the singularity of his style:

Come non lavoro. Che dà egual frutto, a momenti, nella vicenda oscillante d'uno spirito fugitivo e aleatorio, chiamato dall'improbabile altrettanto e forse più che dal probabile: da una puerizia atterrita e dal dolore e dalla disciplina militare e di scuola delabante poi verso il nulla, col suo tesoro d'oscurità e d'incertezze. (*VM*, 427)

[How I do not work. Which gives equal results, at times, in the unsteady life of a transitory and alterable spirit, summoned by the improbable more perhaps than by the probable: by a terrifying childhoood, by grief, and by military and academic discipline stumbling then towards nothingness, with its stock of obscurity and uncertainty.]

This quotation begins an essay, published in *Paragone* in 1949, written by Gadda in response to an invitation extended to several writers to expound on the principles behind their literary practice. It is inscribed, to use the words Contini reserves for all of Gadda's essays, on that threshold of self-destruction ('abissi di tenebra e d'angoscia' [abysses of darkness and angst]) from which, according to Contini, Gadda is saved by his creative genius (Gadda 1963: 14). The experience it describes, because of Gadda's usual restraint before the concrete factuality of his life, hovers on the border between history and myth.

The self which Gadda constructs throughout his fiction can in many respects be termed a 'baroque self,' in that it stretches a life beyond its precise historical limits into infinite partitions or inflections. This life does not crystallize in independent phases or points, but blends into a series of figures inscribed in propositions predicated on an individual subject. The numerous reflections on the authorial self that we find in Gadda's writings, from Captain Gaddüs and Engineer Baronfo to Gonzalo Pirobutirro, Don Ciccio Ingravallo, and Alì Oco De Madrigal, constitute a folded-out personal unity, a repository of propositions that contribute to the modelling of a fully shaped allegorical figure, a figure that both reveals and contains (protects) the author.

An approach to Gadda from the standpoint of his baroque aesthetic is justified by the importance the baroque holds both in the genesis of modernity and, in particular, for post-structuralist criticism. In this respect, Gilles Deleuze's *Le Pli. Leibniz et le Baroque* (1988) carries special weight because it elaborates the notion of a neo-baroque[5] in relation to one of Gadda's more important philosophical sources.[6]

Deleuze's discussion of Leibniz's philosophy provides some valuable insights into Gadda's own readings of the *Monadologie* and the *Théodicée*, particularly into what Deleuze calls 'the baroque concept of the story.' Deleuze argues that Leibniz's philosophy can be conceived as an allegory of the world. He regards the *Théodicée* as a foundational narrative of the Roman Empire, in which Sextus and Lucretia, rather than being symbolic abstractions of particular concepts, contain those concepts within their figures; their story 'combines figures, inscriptions or propositions, individual subjects or points of view with their propositional concepts' (1993: 127). For Deleuze, Leibniz has thus provided a paradigm for the baroque story: 'The baroque introduces a new kind of story in which [...] description replaces the object, the concept becomes narrative, and the subject becomes point of view or subject of expression" (ibid). Although these traits may be found in all allegories, they stand out in Gadda's work as distinctive formal features that make possible the absolute conflation of subjective and objective perspectives, a *modus operandi* that produces the *Omnis in unum* effect of stories enclosed one in the other as different modulations of the same thematic refrain. The basic unity of *La cognizione del dolore* and *Quer pasticciaccio brutto de via Merulana* consists, in fact, not in the narration of realities that form a relevant body of knowledge, but rather in the descriptive process that engulfs those realities, suffocating them to the extent that they drop out altogether as signifying elements. Georg Lukàcs's well-known distinction between narrating and describing would certainly not obtain in Gadda's case. For description in Gadda is neither digression nor static contemplation; nor is it a question of whether description is extrinsic (naturalism) or intrinsic (realism) to his plots. The simple reason is that there are no plots in Gadda, no centre from which the narrator can stray. In his narratives, description of the object world is itself the story and thus acts as a surrogate for another story that has been withdrawn or repressed. Description also takes the place of plot and character, overturning the classical functions of setting and mood. For example, *La cognizione del dolore* begins with what looks like an attempt to establish a narrative frame of reference (the setting for the action). Yet the described world of Maradagàl is so replete with objects that attract the narrator's eye that it cannot hold its own as the centre of attention. As soon as it is evoked, it gives way in rapid succession to a multitude of solicitations. Take, for example, the idea of crop diseases, which sets in motion a description that exceeds the objective referential frame, taking on a life of its own:

Paventata, piú che ogni altra [malattia], la ineluttabile 'Peronospera bazanvoisi' del Cattaneo: essa opera, nella misera pianta, a un disseccamento e sfarinamento delle radicine e del fusto, proprio nei mesi dello sviluppo: e lascia ai disperati e agli affamati, invece del granone, un tritume simile a quello che lascia dietro di sé il tarlo, o il succhiello, in un trave di rovere. In talune plaghe bisogna poi fare i conti anche con la grandine. A quest'altro flagello, in verità, non è particolarmente esposta la involuta pannocchia del banzavois, ch'è una specie di granoturco dolciastro proprio a quel clima. Clima o cielo, in certe regioni, altrettanto grandinifero che il cielo incombente su alcune mezze pertiche della nostra indimenticabile Brianza: terra, se mai altra, meticolosamente perticata. (571)

[Feared above all others was the ineluctable 'Peronospera banzavoisi' mentioned by Cattaneo: it causes, in the hapless plant, a drying and crumbling of the little roots and stem in the very months of development: and for the desperate and the hungry, it leaves, instead of corn, a powder similar to that left behind by the termite, or a gimlet, in an oak beam. In certain regions hail also had to be taken into consideration. This last scourge, to tell the truth, doesn't have a great effect on the wrapped ear of the banzavois, which is a kind of sweetish maize proper to that climate. Climate or sky, in certain regions, as hail bearing as the sky that hangs over certain half-acres of our own unforgettable Brianza: a land, if there ever was one, carefully acred out.][7]

Using Deleuze's terminology, we can refer to such inflections in the narration as 'descriptive folds.' The line they determine is not finite; that is, the solicitation is not delimited or partitioned in the form of an illustration or particularization of a general idea, but instead moves between the surface of the narrative and some interior space, or subtext, bringing the spirit of the author in contact with the matter summoned to express it. It forms, in other words, a texture that bridges the dichotomy between author and text. Description in Gadda is then a means of reconciling the inside and the outside, the high and the low (Deleuze 1988: 35), spheres, independent of one another, that through description are integrated.

In terms of literary architecture, Gaddian description is the façade consisting of an explosive, exacerbated language; a complicated decoration shrouding a closed interiority, incapable of direct speech or communication. In La cognizione such a process is materialized in the meta-textual referent of the Pirobutirro villa, whose walls contain literally the autobiographical soul of the narrative. Behind them, the inseparable existences of Mother and Son unfold and fold out into the world. Put succinctly, the autobiographical object, the self as centre and principle of unity, is replaced by description, intertwined into the labyrinth of matter; it unwinds descriptively from the standpoint of others, including the narrator, who takes leave of his own autobiographical identity in adopting the third person to force a separation between himself and Gonzalo. The motif of the Nistitúos folds out into the bizarre, carnivalesque account of the life of Gaetano Palumbo alias Pedro Mahagones alias Manganones, which in turn folds into the story of the merchant, which in turn folds into the description of Peppa, Beppina, and Pina, then into that of the villas ('Di ville, di ville!; di villette …').

Within these descriptive folds we find the multifold 'pleats of matter,' an indefinite stretching out of the description's constituent parts to form a labyrinth. These pleats envelop what has now become the object of narration, forming 'little vortices in a maelstrom' (Deleuze 1988: 8). To illustrate fully the stylistic complexity of such a procedure would exceed the limits of this introduction. Let it suffice to look at one unit or 'pleat' (itself relatively lengthy) of the story of Gaetano Palumbo (Pedro), the Nistitúos guard assigned to watch over the Pirobutirro villa: the physical description of his face:

Era, sopra la corpulente imponenza della persona, e sul collo chiuso dell'uniforme, una faccia larga e paterna dai corti baffi, a spazzola e rossi, dal naso breve, diritto: gli occhi affossati, piccoli, lucidi, assai mobili con faville acutissime e d'una luce di lama nello sguardo, cui la visiera attenuava ma non poteva spegnere interamente. Quando levava il berretto, come a lasciare vaporare la cabeza, allora la fronte appariva alta, ma piú stretta degli zigomi, e fuggiva con alcune modulazioni di tinta nella cupola del cranio calvo, bianco, e, a onor del vero, assai pulito, cioè senza lentiggine di crassume e di polveri impastati assieme. Allora, senza visiera, gli occhi rimanevano soli al comando, ferivano l'interlocutore con una espressione di dover assolutamente pagare qualche cosa, una specie di multa virtuale, per legge: perché così voleva la legge: ricevendone in adeguato concambio uno scontrino rosa, o cilestro, come ricevuta, spiccato da un libercoletto a matrici ch'egli sapeva estrarre da una tasca laterale della giubba con una naturalezza straordinaria. Tutti, o almeno quasi tutti, d'altronde, nella zona di Lukones, s'erano messi d'impegno e di buona volontà, visto che pagare avevano pagato, a farsi un'idea di quelle pericolose ronde nel buio: e avevano finito per mandar giú anche l'importanza e la delicatezza dell'incarico che gravava sulle sue spalle, per quanto è lunga e buia la notte, e tutti ormai ci credevano, all'importanza: dacché non sempre la buona fama di un uomo, nel Sud America, o la notorietà di un funzionario, dipende dalla inutilità delle sue mansioni. (CD, 576)

[It was, above the imposing corpulence of his person, and resting on the buttoned collar of his uniform, a broad and paternal face with a clipped red bush of a moustache, and a short, straight nose: the eyes were sunken, tiny, glistening, darting, with the bright sparks of a blade's flash in his gaze, attenuated by his visor, which however couldn't extinguish it entirely. When he took off his cap, as if to let his cabeza steam, his forehead then appeared, high but narrower than the cheekbones, and receding with some modulations of hue into the dome of the white, bald cranium, which was, truth to tell, very clean, that is without freckles of dust and grease kneaded together. Then, visorless, his eyes remained alone in command; they wounded the interlocutor with an expression of demand and expectation; one had the sensation of absolutely having to pay something, a sort of virtual fine, by law – because this is what the law required – receiving in return for it a pink or pale blue chit, as a receipt, detached from a little book with counter chits which he could draw from a side-pocket of his tunic with extraordinary naturalness. Everyone, or almost everyone, in the Lukones area had tried hard and with all the will in the world, since they had paid up, to form an idea of those perilous rounds in the dark: and they also had swallowed the importance and the delicacy of the assignment that weighed on his shoulders, through all the length and darkness of the night, and everybody now believed in it, in this importance: since a man's good name, in South America, or an official's notoriety doesn't always derive from the uselessness of his duties. (*AG*, 10–11)]

The units of this description are stages that allow the reader to pass from one level to another: from the material phenomenon (the face) to the inside (the soul) to the outside (the world). Each unit contains several subunits (smaller pleats, potentially infinite in number). What is baroque about the portrait is that each of its units (or subunits) is an open linkage, not governed by any one principle of narrative identity that fixes it with a particular function in relation to an overriding (metaphysical) unity. Rather each unit is a kind of vein that gives definition to an unfinished block of marble – the metaphor is also Deleuze's – but does not determine its form; its destiny is repetition and endless proliferation. Pedro's story can go on indefinitely, given Gadda's belief in the interrelatedness of things and the fact that it contains, instead of one specific object, only differential relations. In fact, when it incorporates the story of the cloth merchant, displacing itself onto another potentially endless trajectory, the authorial voice comically intervenes, stating it is time to stop ('esaurire questa stupida storia e potercene sbarazzare una volta per tutte' [580] – exhaust this stupid story and be rid of it once and for all [15]).

Another distinguishing feature of this description is that it is infinitely receptive to authorial solicitation and thus capable of being deflected spontaneously. This trait is sustained through the unspecified citation of a stylistic model (Manzoni),[8] repeatedly destabilized through comic interruption (e.g., 'Quando levava il berretto, come a lasciare vaporare la cabeza, allora la fronte appariva alta ...') or through authorial glosses ('a onor del vero,' 'perché così voleva la legge,' 'o almeno quasi tutti') that establish the parodic tone of the description.

In *Quer pasticciaccio* the same holds true. Description operates to transform what is planned as a detective story, thus what is meant to conform to certain laws of equilibrium and order, into a pastiche. The elements of plot, all present initially in the text, are continually made subject to secondary linkages that end up by destabilizing a seemingly organic structure, converting it into incoherent aggregates that depend for their form on authorial impulses conditioned by the solicitations evoked by material references, the most notorious being that of Mussolini and fascism. Contrary to traditional crime fiction, *Quer pasticciaccio* proliferates, rather than condenses, meaning. The text exceeds its pre-established frame, radiates in every direction, invading, it seems, every surface. The generic convention, according to which the formal coordinates (crime, criminal, detective, collectivity) define the intersecting lines of final causes and moral necessity, converges with a material universe of disorder. Each of these coordinates is assimilated to an infinite curvature of inflection (Deleuze 1988: 101) in a way that every one of them expresses a complex of differential relations, a general diffusion of meanings within a structure in which meanings are normally condensed. This is what Calvino is referring to when he describes *Quer pasticciaccio* as an inquiry into the world conceived as a 'system of systems' in which 'every element of a system contains within it another system; each individual system in turn is linked to a genealogy of systems. A change in any particular element results in a breakdown of the whole.'[9] It is useful to emphasize, however, that each element of the convention or system, if considered abstractly, is a world onto itself, a designated zone of meaning and inquiry, a pre-established harmony,' which submits to the impression, and thus expression, of authorial impulse. Hence, through description, the object of narration spills over the boundaries of its frame (take, for example, the initial description of Don Ciccio) to join a broader cycle of meaning.

To illustrate the relationship of concept to object in Gadda, it is useful to consider, albeit schematically, the composition of the objective world in realist fiction, and how such a world is expressed through its characters. Manzoni's Don Abbondio, for example – a figure, incidentally, particularly dear to Gadda – is one among many object realities the author creates to convey a particular sense of the world. As the personification of moral weakness and private interest, his form constitutes a particular frame that, existing side by side with other frames, operates to complete the systematic expression of the world as Manzoni sees it. Although Don Abbondio interacts with other characters, he retains his specific difference and never encroaches on their space. He speaks in a voice totally commensurate with his moral figure, and in his actions combines momentary reality and universal concept. The narration of this concept (Abbondio in all of his negative and lovable qualities) is, of course, the character in all its being and action, distinct in quality and extension from all the other characters and subsumed to Manzoni's moral and aesthetic ideas. The narrative, or story, constitutes, in other words, a universal frame that incorporates particular concepts of reality; the horizontal axis is centred in the vertical.

In Gadda's baroque world, the individualized realist frame loses all of its autonomy. The unity of the one in the many is replaced by a point of view that projects downward from the top, permeating the text at every level. What appear as fragments or unspecified spaces are coordinated by means of the overriding concept of entanglement. This gives rise to a vision of the world in which all boundaries are transgressed and where the authorial self is externalized into a series of figures and events.

In *La cognizione* the concept (of entanglement) that engulfs the narrative is conveyed first and foremost by the novel's title. For it directs the reader's attention to the subject in which the faculty of acquiring knowledge resides, while at the same time emphasizing knowledge as process: the continual perception of the knowing subject. At the same time, it posits the existence of a referent that defies specification because it is one and the same with life itself. Hence the title, rather than referring to a particular object of narration, evokes the unique condition of the point of view from which that narration will unfold. There is an inevitable cause of human suffering that the subject alone can understand: he alone has the gift of deep perception into a complicated and confused reality; he alone has the insights and the power to extend his concept of chaos into narration .[10]

In *Quer pasticciaccio*, we see even more clearly how entanglement gives texture to the narration and thus constitutes its unifying principle. Right from the beginning the narrative shows its own capacity for radiating in all directions in the search for some one thing that will define a specific object of perception. But immediately we realize that such a procedure has been sanctioned by the point of view of Don Ciccio, the very character it is engaged in describing:

Sosteneva, fra l'altro, che le inopinate catastrofi non sono mai la consequenza o l'effetto che dir si voglia d'un unico motivo, di una causa al singolare: ma sono come un vortice, un punto di depressione ciclonica nella coscienza del mondo, verso cui hanno cospirato tutta una molteplicità di causali convergenti.[11]

[He maintained, among other things, that unforeseen catastrophes are never the consequence or the effect, if you prefer, of a single motive, of *a* single singular; but they are rather like a whirlpool, a cyclonic point of depression in the consciousness of the world, to which a whole multitude of converging causes have contributed.][12]

Hence the narrative point of view is taken from the detective whose work is destined never to finish because, like that of the narrator, his philosophy raises the fabric of the world up to infinity. The 'nodo,' 'groviglio,' 'garbuglio,' or 'gnommero' can never be disentangled, but just folded out endlessly. The narration, in other words, because it is one and the same with its own guiding concept, can never be concluded, but only interrupted.[13]

If we shift our focus from the concept that becomes the narration to the subject of the narration, we see that the authorial point of view and the subject of narrative are one and the same. The manner in which they are linked, however, is not typical of either classical autobiographical narratives or 'autobiografismo.'

In using the term 'subject' I am referring to the text's controlling consciousness, the point of view that produces the reality to which it subjects the reader. In other words, this 'subject' creates the text's ideology by providing the knowledge necessary for placing the reader in a position appropriate to an understanding of the story. It does so by elaborating a discourse that gives the story its particular form. The story's discursive organization is then subject to a meta discourse which supervises and regulates the development of the elements and procedures it adopts in order to convey its vision. Such a 'vision' in classical narrative is motivated by a desire for unity.[14] In traditional autobiographical narrative the same relation between discourse and story holds true. The self (or the surrogate that stands in for the self in 'autobiografismo') that speaks is the subject that organizes the text to give it its patina of truth and spontaneity.

In Gadda, the controlling subject occupies a position of control, but it cannot in effect control the meaning it produces. The position of the author is generally assumed by the narrator who, while attempting to organize the materials of his story, cannot distance himself sufficiently from them in order to promote the illusion of either objectivity or, by contrast, subjective involvement. His attachment to the objects of his narration can be best described as 'schizophrenic.' The object world is for him the source of confusion. It contains a multiplicity of positions which he cannot control by excluding or absorbing. His status as narrator is problematic because he cannot sustain the discourse he has initiated. And it is equally problematic because it cannot maintain its position of control. As a result, the authorial voice, or meta discourse, to which the narrator's point of view is subject, becomes itself subjected to the material impulses it has generated, literally left to the mercy of the world it has created. Put differently, the inner world of the author prevents the novel from being written for the simple reason that it undermines any and all pretensions to unity or resolution. The effect is that the subject has difficulty focusing on the object; it cannot establish the correct distance from which to view the object; it is unable to establish a criterion of relevance that may serve to underpin its ideology. While Gadda's texts express conservative political and social beliefs, they do so without a principle of ideological transcription, that is to say, those beliefs are not represented 'innocently' as reality or truth. The breakdown in the construction of subjectivity is a breakdown in the epistemology that makes ideological closure possible. In the baroque conflation of the subject with the subject of expression, the burden of truth is borne not by a controlling consciousness, but rather by expression.

Through expression, the object of narration in Gadda takes on a new status. It no longer refers back to a content that has been given an objective shape. Instead it exists in a continual state of modulation determined by its convergence with the narrating subject. The object is, in other words, at the mercy of the teller of the story, who envelops it in the constant flux of his moods and impulses. The result of this diffusion of the subjective viewpoint into the object is the transformation of the character into a labyrinth or knot.[15]

To illustrate this process let us take the figures of Son and Mother in the second chapter of Part Two of La cognizione. The narrator begins by describing an image of Gonzalo: his silhouette as seen on the terrace from the open French door of the villa: 'L'alta figura di lui si disegnò nera nel vano della porta-finestra, di sul terrazzo, come l'ombra d'uno sconosciuto' (*CD*, 685). (His tall form was outlined, black, in the frame of the French window, from the terrace, like the shadow of a stranger [*AG*, 148]). The initial effect of an objective perspective established by a would-be omniscient eye is immediately lost by the incorporation into its position of the mother's emotional response at the sight of her son, whom she regards as a stranger in her house. The narration then folds out into a wholly lyrical reference: 'Dioscuri splendidi sopra una fascia d'amaranto, lontana, nel quadrante di bellezza e di conoscenza: fraternità salva!' (ibid) (Splendid Dioscuri over a stripe of amaranth, distant, in the quadrant of beauty and of knowledge: saved fraternity! [ibid]). The narrator has now become the dark figure in the window, who, gazing at the constellation Gemini, is reminded of the immortality shared by both Castor and Pollux, whereas he, Gonzalo, unlike Pollux, cannot intervene to bring his dead brother back to life. The narrator has then encroached on both the space of the Mother, who desperately needs to relate to her son, and the space of Gonzalo, who is obsessed with the death of his brother; he has forfeited his potentially strong position on the outside because he cannot separate his frame of interrogation from that of his characters. At the same time, he does not relinquish a certain degree of distance afforded him by the authorial perspective he voices. While the lyrical reference to the myth of Castor and Pollux evokes an experience on the borders of the ineffable, it does so parodically by mimicking Gonzalo (and Gadda's) need to sublimate his grief into literature. This parodic instance is prefigured by the equally parodic insertion at the beginning of the passage of 'di' before 'sul,' which destabilizes the objective description, echoing a procedure common to Leopardi and Carducci. Hence three boundaries are crossed in the space of two sentences: author, narrator, and character are tangled in such a way that it is practically impossible to distinguish one from the other. The tangle becomes even more intricate as the narrator returns to focus on Gonzalo: 'Egli allora entrò, e recava una piccola valigia, la solita, quella di cartone giallo da quaranta centavos, come d'un venditore ambulante di fazzoletti' (685–6). (He came in then, and was carrying a small valise, the usual, the one of yellow cardboard costing forty centavos, like a traveling peddler of handkerchiefs [148].) Now the narrative voice blends with that of the chorus of townspeople, for whom Gonzalo is an eccentric misanthrope, and the image of the travelling pedlar returns as another obsessive reference to what Gonzalo believes is his mother's excessive liberality.

The blurring of perspectives brings together the different worlds that comprise the book (the worlds of Gonzalo, his mother, the doctor-colonel Di Pascuale, the townspeople), resulting in a new kind of harmony that issues from the polytonal recentring of the different viewpoints into one overriding conceptual refrain. From now on, the reader must recognize that, with the narrator, he is trapped within a labyrinth from which there is no exit; it is the labyrinth of authorial consciousness and cognition. As the narrator recounts the mother's need to please her son by proving that the villa is functional, he becomes by degrees at once both character and author. He begins by reflecting what the mother could have been thinking as she prepared supper for her son: that at the slightest provocation he would burst into tirades against everything associated with the villa he so hated. But, as soon as the circuit, so to speak, of the mother's possible thoughts and fears is established, the narrator overloads it with an endless description of the objects of Gonzalo's invectives ('Egli avrebbe colto quel pretesto[...]' 'Avrebbe ripetutamente scorbacchiato[...]' 'Sarebbe trasceso alle bestemmie[...]' [686]) – (He would have seized upon that pretext ... He would have repeatedly ridiculed ... he would have cursed'... [149]), folding thus an apparently objective perspective with distinct frames of reference into an infinite series of converging singularities (the villa and every association that it elicits in Gonzalo's paranoiac consciousness). We witness a vast play of expression which fills the holes of the protagonist's emptiness with a formidable excess:

La Idea Matrice della villa se l'era appropriata quale organo rubente od entelechia prima consustanziale ai visceri, e però inalienabile dalla sacra interezza della persona: quasi armadio od appiccapanni di De Chirico, carnale ed eterno dentro il sognante cuore dei lari. A quella pituita somma, recondita, noumenica, corrispondeva esternamente – gioiello o bargiglio primo fuor dai confini della psiche – la villa obbiettiva, il dato. Operando in lei, durante quarant'anni, gli ormoni infaticabili della anagenesi; ciò che donna prende, in vita lo rende: quella costanza imperterrita, quella felice ignoranza dell'abisso, del paracarro, sicché, dàlli e dàlli, d'un cetriolo, arrivano a incoronar fuori un ingegnere; la formidabile capacità di austione, di immissione dello sproposito nella realtà, che è propria d'alcune meglio di esse; le più deliberate e di più vigoroso intelletto. Tali donne, anche se non sono isteriche, impegnano magari il latte, e la caparbietà di tutta una vita, a costituire in thesaurum certo, storicamente reale, un qualsiasi prodotto d'incontro della umana stupidaggine, il primo che capiti loro fra i piedi, a non dir fra le gambe, il piú vano: simbolo efimero di una emulazione o riverenza od acquisto che conterà nulla: diploma grande, villa, sissignora, piumacchio. C'è poi da aggiungere che il piú degli uomini si comportano tal'e quale come loro. Ed è una proprio delle meraviglie di natura, a volerlo considerare nei modi e nei resultati, questo processo di accumulo della volizione: è l'incedere automatico della sonnambula verso il tuo trionfo-catastrofe: da un certo momento in poi l'isteria del ripicco perviene a costituire la loro sola ragione d'essere, di tali donne, le adduce alla menzogna, al reato: e allora il vessillo dell'inutile, con la grinta buggerona della falsità, è portato avanti, avanti, sempre piú ostinatamente, sempre piú inutilmente, avverso la rabbia disperata della controparte. Sopravviene la tenebra liberatrice, che a tutte parti rimedia. (687)

[The Matrix Idea of the villa she had appropriated for herself as a rubescent organ or prime entelechy consubstantial with the womb, and therefore inalienable from the sacred wholeness of her person: like a wardrobe or hatrack of De Chirico, carnal and external within the dreaming heart of the lares. To that pituitary sum, recondite, noumenical, there corresponded externally – jewel or prime cock crest beyond the confines of the psyche – the objective villa, the datum. Operating in her, during forty years, were the tireless hormones of anagenesis – what woman takes, in life she gives back – that unperturbed constancy, that happy ignorance of the abyss, of the curbstone, so that, never say die, from pumpkin head, they manage to produce an engineer; the formidable capacity for absorption, for introduction of absurdity into reality, which is characteristic of some of the best of women – the most resolute, the most vigorous of intellect. Such women, even if they aren't hysterical, impound their milk, and the stubbornness of a whole life, to constitute a thesaurus certain, historically real, a commonplace product of the encounter with human stupidity: the first that they find at their feet, not to say between their legs, the vainest: ephemeral symbol of an emulation or a reverence or an acquisition which will count for nothing: large diploma, villa, yes Madame, plume. It must be added also that the majority of men behave exactly like them. And it is really one of the wonders of nature, if you choose to consider it in its methods and results, this process of accumulation of volition. It is automatic progress of the somnambulist toward her triumph-catastrophe: from a certain moment on, the hysteria of pique succeeds in forming their sole reason for existence; in such women, it leads them to falsehood, to crime, and then the banner of the useless, with the fraudulent mug of falsity, is borne forward, forward, more and more obstinately, more and more uselessly, against the desperate anger of the other side. The liberating darkness arrives, which remedies all sides. (150–1)]

The development of this passage, which for reasons of space I have excerpted from a much larger context, depends on the subordination of the narrative (and historical) truth (the mother's pride and identification with the villa) to the creative potential of that truth. The truth holds what Deleuze calls an 'infinité de petites perceptions' (1988: 122), the value of which consists not in whether they are true, but in the fact that they gain privileged status in expression. Samples of the perceptions constituting the passage just cited include: 'La Idea Matrice': the villa as mother or womb; 'l'organo rubente': villa as phallus; 'entelechia prima consustanziale ai visceri': the mother's desire for self-fulfillment in the villa; 'armadio od appiccapanni di De Chirico': the kinds of inalienable objects that occupy the domestic space of the villa, which in De Chirico's art are metaphysical values; 'pituita somma': hormonic fatality perceived as noumenon: the villa as thing in itself; 'anagenesis': the villa as compensation for the loss of a son (Gadda/Gonzalo's brother); 'costanza imperterrita [...] ingegnere': the mother's predisposition to surrender to the phallus.

These perceptions are not meant as a rational illustration of a general theme or idea through particular examples; they do not serve to define the relation between villa and mother; nor are they qualities of a physical reality that excite the mind of the narrator. Rather they find unity only in the narrative unconscious; they are in effect unconscious perceptions articulated by free association: the folds of the villa/mother as idea embedded in the monadic inner world of a hysterical subject. They rise from the depths of his being and take on the quality of hallucinations.[16]

The autobiographical subject in all of its inflections cannot then disentangle itself from its inner world of a 'dolore' it cannot explain but only express. At the same time it is aware of the liability accompanying its own expression: namely, the impulse to dissolve the grief into literature which for Gadda is both expression and disguise. Gadda's profound awareness of his own potential for literary entrapment is one of the most distinctive features of his art. It enables him to exit, however slightly, from the anxieties and obsessions that characterize his paranoia and thus to take some degree of distance from his own baroque expressionism. It makes possible the comedy and the spectacle, the thorough materialization of systems within systems.

In conclusion, to understand Gadda's baroque, one must keep in mind Gadda's stated premise that the universe is baroque, while rejecting the implication that his texts are that world's mimetic transcription. Gadda ceases to transmit the exterior world at the very moment he engages in self-reflection and inspection. Yet in so doing he takes a position at the opposite extreme of that espoused by contemporary theoreticians and practitioners of the neo-baroque. By exposing the self as the sole arbiter of meaning, he cannot move beyond his own chaotic representations. The vibrations and oscillations of the narrative psyche that, as we have seen, shatter traditional language boundaries and framing structures are not made to exemplify in the least an indeterminate process of meaning production. Rather the complexity that Gadda's self- referentiality highlights is the reduction of the world and of all its chaos and fragments to authorial intention and, therefore, to one infinitely communicable experience: the quintessential experience of 'wordless pain within the monad,' as Fredric Jameson writes in reference to Edward Munch's painting *The Scream*, the cathartic projection and externalization of 'gesture or cry, as desperate communication and the outward dramatization of inward feeling' (1992: 11–12).

2

Baroque Solitude: Disillusion and the Ruins of War

Is there a real moment in time when the world collapses into fragments and the agony begins? Gadda has often cited the problems of his childhood, mainly his family's uncertain financial status, as the principal cause of his malaise, and criticism advisedly has traced, with relative success, the many images of torment and trauma present in his work to their autobiographical matrix. Attempts to penetrate Gadda's inner world by means of psychoanalysis have produced some compelling readings, but also, inevitably, several difficulties, among which the attempt to find a ground for Gadda's distinctive manner of writing is dominant. This chapter concerns itself with Gadda's experience as a combatant in the First World War, repeatedly singled out by him as *the* traumatic event of his life.

Gadda fought in the war as a second lieutenant, assigned to the Fifth Alpine Division infantry, and was imprisoned, after the battle of Caporetto, at Celle Lager in Hanover. Gadda's record of his war experience is contained in the *Giornale di guerra e di prigionia*,[1] a diary he kept from 24 August 1915 through December 1919 and which he refers to as 'testimonianza e confessione' (testimony and confession) of the 'sanguinoso pandemonio della storia "europea" di allora'[2] (bloody pandemonium of the then 'European' history). *Il castello di Udine,* a collection of memories and polemics, harbours reflections on the war and its aftermath formulated at a distance of more than ten years,[3] while themes associated with the war extend in multiple directions, constituting a luminous horizon against which we can see come into being Gadda's unique baroque manner and sensibility.

The *Giornale* contains a mode of correspondence which defines the author's life at the level of morality. The pressures the forces of war exert on the young Gadda fix his place in the world as a solitary individual, dissociated from the sphere of ordinary existence. The journal deals with a situation in which the war is seen both as a national necessity ('Ho presentito la guerra come una dolorosa necessità nazionale' [CU, 142]; I considered the war to be a painful national necessity), a way of preserving a civilization and way of life ('L'Europe aux anciens parapets'),[4] and a force which lays bare the moral ruin of Italy. The experience recorded is, from a personal standpoint, exceptional. By seizing on it, Gadda not only captures the event of his time, but also develops a technique for organization and control, which becomes a medium for the representation and the legitimization of the self.

So it is with scientific precision that he registers his daily routine as a soldier, indicating even the slightest change in schedules or procedures and describing in minute detail every aspect of his physical and social life. The position of encampments, battle strategies, and the character of his fellow soldiers are made the object of constant scrutiny. Introspection leads gradually to self-portraiture: gentle and mannered, naturally indolent and melancholic, timid and introverted, highly susceptible to practical jokes, and fearful of not withstanding the hardships and risks of war on account of his physical weaknesses. Gadda sees as his major problem an ultra-sensitive nervous system, to which he attributes his mania for order and his intolerance of all kinds of irrational behaviour. He is engaged in a sacred war; his actions are thus profoundly moral, as is the calm reverence he displays for military rules ('Il Gaddüs è il pio credente nella legge, e nella sua continua sanzione' [GGP, 452]; Gaddüs is a pious believer in the law and in its continuous sanction) and his unbending faith in the logic he believes inherent in reality. The figure that emerges from these entries is that of the neurotic idealist, fascinated by the world as it should be and intolerant of anything that contradicts his ideals and expectations. Gadda's self-portrait, while exhibiting his submission to authority and hierarchy, underlines the presence of a self-willed, independent individual, a solitary, depressed soul entrapped amid the masses.[5]

The journal delineates a structure of instability. From contact with the reality of his environment, Gadda realizes that the world of the Other, in which he must live and survive, is not governed by reason ('lontano dalla sapienza e dal metodo dell'analisi, di cui Manzoni è insigne maestro e profondo esemplificatore' [GGP, 456]; distant from the wisdom and analytic method of which Manzoni is the renowned master and penetrating illustrator). The knowing process therefore is one of disenchantment, the proverbial *desengaño* of the Spanish baroque. The world is unstable, and largely unbearable, because it does not conform to the ideal – hence the subject's alienation.

The precision with which Gadda transcribes even the most insignificant aspects of his physical environment conceals, from his very first entries, a hint of desperation. His private world of material objects, the contents of his room, which for the neurotic constitutes a fixed point of reference, does not meet with his expectations, lined as it is with functional disorder:

La camera che qui abito è a Sud Ovest, la migliore esposizione, a dieci metri dal quartiere, ed è stanza d'angolo con due finestre: è alta poco più di due metri, a quadrilatero irregolare, bianca, pulita, ma molto fredda e senza stufa né camino [...] La catinella, piccola, in ferro, con dell'acqua gelida, è posata sopra uno sgabello. Vi è uno specchio, un tavolo, un cassettone, due sedie, il letto e il tavolino da notte. Il letto è un'ottomana, corta, in cui devo stare rannicchiato. (*GGP*, 493)

[The room I inhabit has a southeast exposure, located ten metres from the centre of the camp. It is a corner room with two windows; it is the shape of an irregular rectangle with a height of slightly more that two metres; it is painted white and is clean, but very cold and without either a stove or a fireplace ... The small, metal basin full of ice-cold water rests upon a stool. There is a mirror, a table, a chest of drawers, two chairs, a bed and night table. The bed is a short ottoman on which I sleep curled up.]

Gadda believed the war was not only a sacred cause, but also an arena which would give him the opportunity to test his genius and thereby to elevate himself above common humanity. But instead of fostering self-redemption, the war caused a build-up of internal pressures, bringing to the surface latent traumas. As the months pass, Gadda becomes more and more aware that he was doomed to a monotonous life and that his potential for greatness had been undermined by a cruel fate. The style of his notes often reflect this disenchantment, underlining the impossibility on Gadda's part of serene and detached observation of the outside world, the kind of rational perspective he attributed to his beloved Manzoni. Objectivity fails him because reality has proven to be a total disappointment:

Sento che i più cari legami si dissolvono, che il maledetto destino vuol divellermi dalle pure origini della mia anima e privarmi delle mie forze più pure, per fare di me un uomo comune, volgare, tozzo, bestiale, borghese, traditore di sé stesso, italiano, 'adatto all'ambiente'. Tutto ha congiurato contro la mia grandezza, e prima di ogni cosa il mio animo, debole, docile, facile ad esser preso dalle ragioni altrui; poiché in tutti, anche nei più miserabili, v'è un po'di ragione, o almeno la logica della realtà. Se la realtà avesse avuto minor forza sopra di me, oppure se la realtà fosse di quelle che consentono la grandezza (Roma, Germania), io sarei un uomo che vale qualcosa. Ma la realtà di questi anni, salve alcune fiamme generose e fugaci, è merdosa: e in esso mi sento immedesimare ed annegare. (*GGP*, 863)

[I feel my closest ties dissolve and my cursed destiny wants to tear me away from the pure origins of my spirit and deprive me of my best qualities, so that I can become a common man, vulgar, small, brutish, bourgeois, self-traitor, Italian, 'adapted to the environment.' Everything has plotted against my greatness, and above all my own spirit, weak [as it is], docile, easily convinced by the reasoning of others, because in everyone, even the most miserable, there is some reason, or at least the logic of reality. If reality had less power over me, or if reality were of the kind that consents to greatness (Rome, Germany), I would be a man worth something. But reality in these years, with the exception of some generous and fleeting moments, has been shit: in it I feel immersed and drowning.]

From a psychological standpoint, this passage illustrates the hold that the outside world has on Gadda, and his inability to be indifferent to its negative movement. But still more important is the logic that regulates such a relationship. Between the ideal and the real, we find no mediating element; the negative and positive extremes of existence are frozen in place without any possibility of synthesis: there is the subject as ideal (the moral greatness it envisions for itself) and the subject as real (its plunge into the commonplace). Without the possibility of resolving the antithesis, the subject is already split, given over to the Other. The logic of ambivalence (between the good and the contaminated self) affects the mode of self-representation. Because of the power of reality on his psyche, the authority of the Other over him, Gadda cannot reflect on himself as the centre or controlling consciousness of his experiences. Otherness is always present and absent, as is the true self. This explains why in the *Giornale* the real terms of the war (enemy, opposing ideologies, battle strategies, etc.) are forfeited, as the conflict turns quickly into a struggle between Gadda and his immediate environment. Every external provocation sparks anxieties generated by a conscience tortured by inactivity and incomprehension: 'Troppo gli aspetti non sereni dell'ambiente si stampano nel mio animo agghiacciandolo di uno sgomento insuperabile e togliendogli la facoltà della reazione' (GGP, 503); Too often the disquieting features of the environment stamp themselves on my soul, freezing it in an insuperable paralysis and depriving it of the faculty to react). It also explains why his journal entries, like the universe of the baroque, are weighted with numerous forms which fill the emptiness left by the exhausted self.

The writing subject has before it the chaos of the world which it recreates through declamation and enumeration. Anger ignites a declamatory prose in which objects are chaotically enumerated and incongruously juxtaposed in order to reveal the comic absurdity of those signs of Otherness that are now part of the subject's private sphere:

Che porca rabbia, che porchi italiani. Quand'è che i miei luridi compatrioti di tutte le classi, di tutti i ceti, impareranno a tener ordinato il proprio tavolino di lavoro? A non ammonticchiarvi le carte d'ufficio insieme alle lettere della mantenuta, insieme al cestino della merenda, insieme al ritratto della propria nipotina, insieme al giornale, insieme all'ultimo romanzo, all'orario delle ferrovie, alle ricevute del calzolaio, alla carta per pulirsi il culo, al cappello sgocciolante, alle forbici delle unghie, al portafoglio privato, al calendario fantasia? Quando, quando? Quand'è che questa razza di maiali, di porci, di esseri capaci soltanto di imbruttire il mondo col disordine e con la prolissità dei loro atti sconclusionati, proverrà alle attitudini dell'ideatore e del costruttore, sarà capace di dare al seguito delle proprie azioni un legame logico? (GGP, 574)

[Damn these Italian pigs! When will my filthy compatriots from every class and social group learn to keep their work table in order. When will they learn not to pile up official papers together with letters from their mistresses, together with picnic baskets, together with photographs of their nieces, newspapers, latest novels, train schedules, shoe repair receipts, paper with which they wipe their asses, rain soaked caps, fingernail clippers, wallets, pin-up calendars? When? When will this race of pigs, of people capable only of making the world ugly with disorder and with the prolixity of their purposeless actions, when will they become thinkers and builders, when will they be capable of giving a logical explanation to their actions?]

And further on:

La nostra anima stupida, porca, cagna, bastarda, superficiale, asinesca tiene per dignità personale il dire 'io faccio quello che voglio; non ho padroni'. Questo si chiama fierezza, libertà, dignità. Quando i superiori ti dicono di tosarti perché i pidocchi non ti popolino testa e corpo, tu, italiano ladro, dici: 'io non mi toso, sono un uomo libero'. Quando un generale passa in prima linea, come passò Bloise, e si lamenta con ragione delle merde sparse dovunque, tu, italiano escremento, dici che il generale si occupa di merde[...] L'egoismo cretino dell'italiano fa di tutto una questione personale. (578)

[Our stupid, pig-like, bitch-like, bastardly, superficial, asinine mind equates with personal dignity the saying 'I do what I want; I have no bosses.' This is pride, dignity, freedom. When your superiors tell you to shave your head and body so that lice don't crawl all over you, you, bloody minded Italian, say: 'I will not shave my head and body, I'm a free man.' When a general inspects our camp, like Bloise did, and complains with good reason of the turds strewn everywhere, you. Italian shit head, say that the general is concerned with shit ... The Italian's idiotic egoism reduces everything to a personal question.]

These passages are characterized by what Christine Buci-Glucksmann has called a 'regress of reality' (1994: 134). Since the chaotic world provides no reference whatsoever for the author's identity, he enacts a process of repetitive captivation that paradoxically mirrors the slipping away of the self. The otherness of the world is energized through enumeration, a technique which, while intent on capturing a non-essential, fragmentary reality, shows that the speaking subject is incapable of mastering that reality, imprinting his identity on it, and thus attempting to exhaust it of its expressive potential, at the very moment it eludes the subject's grasp, folding out, or regressing, infinitely. The war then becomes a representation, a theatre of dramatic movement between the subject and its world: a baroque spectacle.

It cannot escape the reader of Gadda's journal that the technique of enumeration is meant to be a powerful spiritual force. In raising reality up to its extreme, Gadda dematerializes the alien world by making it an extension of his monadic solitude. Every element of the comic disaster he creates, every instance of disorder and banality he lists, accentuates his rational, analytical faculties. This is another way of saying that, with the *Giornale*, Gadda has already become an *author*. The pleasure (and displeasure) he takes in seeing himself as the antithesis or stranger to a race which has deprived him of an Italian homeland, an exile or prisoner in a vulgar world of appearances, the last descendant of the Lombard conquerors, is one and the same with the allegorization of his predicament: the transformation of his precarious existence into an ontology of precariousness, the fictional embodiment of which we find in the character of Gonzalo of *La cognizione del dolore*, the last Hidalgo who 'veniva di sangue barbaro, germanico e unno, oltreché langobardo' (was of barbarian blood, Germanic and Hun, as well as Longobard) and had 'certe manie d'ordine e di silenzio, e nell'odio della carta unta, dei gusci d'ovo, e dell'indugiare sulla porta coi convenevoli' (*CD*, 606–7; certain manias for order and silence, and hatred for greasy paper, egg-shells, and the lingering at the door in formalities). Gonzalo, like Gadda of the *Giornale*, maintained a love–hate relationship with the world, the *Weltsucht* and *Weltflucht* which form the basis of his baroque and expressionistic personality.

The *Giornale* recounts a series of tragedies that can be reduced to specific historical causes, as, for example, the inadequate preparation of the Italian army, Gadda's imprisonment, and the death of his brother. However, at the same time, the persona that emerges from that specific history possesses all the earmarks of a literary figure, one which adds another dimension to Gadda's baroque position. The figure is that of the expressionist hero: extraordinarily sensitive and gifted, he stands out from the masses, but his superiority is also the poison that banishes him into obscurity.[6] The journal's language and style reflect a technique typical of expressionism, for their purpose in transcribing Gadda's war experiences is not to describe or to characterize, but rather to express the urgency and the tension of a particular state of mind. Gadda can be lyrical, and even rhapsodic, in moments of minor friction, and passionate, hyperbolic, and sarcastic when his need to give vent to his anger is inspired by thoughts of a victimized childhood or of some irrational behaviour on the part of his fellow soldiers. The fact that the infantry was not equipped with shoes capable of withstanding the rigours of the battlefield and cold climate, and that soldiers froze to death on account of the lack of warm clothing is sufficient cause for violent invectives which, while they display all the vibrations and oscillations of baroque writing, are wholly expressionistic in their dependence on personal mood and feeling:

Chissà quelle mucche gravide, quegli acquosi pancioni di ministri e di senatori e di direttori e di generaloni; chissà come crederanno di aver proveduto alle sorti del paese con i loro discorsi, visite al fronte, interviste, ecc.– Ma guardino, ma vedano, ma pensino come è calzato il 5. Alpini! Ma Salandra, ma quello balbuziente d'un re, ma quei duchi e quei deputati che vanno 'a vedere le trincee', domandino conto a noi, a me, del come sono calzati i miei uomini: e mi vedrebbe il re, mi vedrebbe Salandra uscir dai gangheri e farmi mettere agli arresti in fortezza[...] Asini, asini, buoi grassi, pezzi da grand hôtel, avana, bagni; ma non guerreri, non pensatori, non ideatori, non costruttori; incapace d'osservazione e d'analisi, ignoranti di cose psicologiche, inabili alla sintesi. (*GGP*, 467–8)

[Who knows how those fat cows, those water-filled bellies of ministers, senators, directors, and decorated generals, who knows how they think they have seen to the needs of our country with their speeches, visits to the front, interviews. Let them come and look and see how my 5th Alpine Division is outfitted. Salandra, that stuttering fool of a king, those dukes and deputies who 'visit the trenches,' let them ask us, ask me, how my men are outfitted, and both the king and Salandra would see me go berserk, arrested and taken away in a straitjacket ... Fools, fools, fat pigs, soap-opera dummies, cigar-smoking, loafers, not warriors, not thinkers, not men of ideas, not builders; incapable of observation and analysis, ignorant of psychology, unable to synthesize.]

By contrast, the tensions and conflicts that torment the neurotic soldier lessen in certain moments, such as when he views the spectacle of mortar and artillery fire light up the night sky. With childlike wonder he watches the horizon explode, as he tries to reproduce stylistically this splendid symphony of sound and colour. Every tension has disappeared, and harmony is re-established amid chaos:

Crepitio di fucili, in aumento, razzi verdi nella pineta, qualche razzo rosso nostro, fuoco di mitragliatrice intermittente, sibilo di shrapnels che di notte scoppiano con un bagliore rosso-livido, qualche fragore di bomba a mano: aumento, maximum, decrescenza. (*GGP*, 553)

[Burst of rifle fire, increasing, green streaks of mortars in the pine forest, some red rockets of our own, intermittent machine-gun fire, the hissing of shrapnel exploding in the night air with a bluish glow, the noise of hand grenades: increase, maximum, decrease.]

In all these passages, there is a notable excess of meaning: the components of the real appear as a superabundance, or overflowing of reality, and the relations established in language are those of insistence (as opposed to coherence or consistency).[7] This baroque feature translates into a perspective for the grotesque. The profusion of difference cannot be left as disorienting fragments spreading in every direction. The discordance must be contained, if it cannot be assimilated; hence, the burden of reason comes face to face with the logic of ambivalence, the stand-off is resolved in the (false) synthesis of the grotesque. The Gaddian grotesque, as we shall see later on, finds its philosophical justification in *Meditazione milanese*. In the war journal, it issues spontaneously from the force of observation, deeply affected by a need to resist the alien presence, even when it is nothing but a reflex image of the self.

At one point in the *Giornale*, Gadda exits momentarily from his diaristic mode and tries his hand at literary description. His object is the image of a captain in the field:

Fra le ondulazioni dolcissime dell'Altipiano, vestite del folto pratíle, il trillo dell'allodola nell'estate è segnato da una nota di apprensione paurosa: un bizzarro spaventapasseri fa venir l'itterizia alle povere creature, avezze al deserto silenzio della vegetazione. Esse lo credono un mostro giallo e maligno, che guarda l'universo con l'occhio dell'augurio funebre: ma egli non è che il vecchio e bravo capitano, a cui il Ministero ha tardato la promozione, a cui la guerra ha cosparso di peli e di sudiciume la faccia, ha impolverato le scarpe e bisunto il vestito. Come un palo sgangherato egli sorge dal verde, le tasche rigonfie di carte e di oggetti di prima necessità, gli abiti di un color frusto e pieni di ogni sorta di pataffie, la giacca corsa da funicelle che reggono il canocchiale e il fischietto e la borsa, la cravatta sollevata del collo, la faccia malata e stanca. Guarda con tristezza la montagna da cui sgorga la rabbia nemica, porta senza gioia la medaglia della campagna coloniale, aspetta senza desiderio la colazione. Mentre le granate fischiano paurosamente egli è ritto nel prato, calmo perché ha fatto quanto poteva per riparare i suoi soldati, e pensa all'ardua prova che il decadere della vita gli serba, dopo tutti i disinganni e le amarezze di questa. Io vedo che la sua cravatta si sposta sempre piú verso l'alto dell'esile collo, lasciando nudo il pomo d'Adamo, e mostrandosi anche piú sudicia di quello che credevo: ascolto alcune sue osservazioni molto sensate, che egli pronuncia con qualche spruzzo di saliva dalla bocca stanca, e mi allontano per non intenerirmi, perché il dar corso a sentimenti troppo affettuosi non è da soldato. Egli mi guarda mentre m'allontano con una faccia che dice: – Te ne vai perché t'ho annoiato? (*GGP*, 561–2)

[Amid the sweetest undulations of the densely green highland, the trill of the wood lark in the summer is marked by a note of fearful apprehension. A bizarre scarecrow riles the poor creatures spoiled by the desert-like silence of the vegetation. They see it as a malicious, yellow monster that surveys the world with a funereal eye. But it is nothing but the good, old captain for whom the Ministry has delayed promotion and whose face the war has covered with hair and dirt, made dusty his shoes and greasy his outfit. Like a wobbly pole he emerges from the green field, his pockets overburdened with papers and objects of prime necessity, his drab uniform decorated with every kind of spot, his jacket traversed by cords that sustain his telescope, whistle, and bag, his tie high on his neck, his face ill and tired. He looks sadly at the mountain from which issues the enemy's rage, he wears without joy the medal of the colonial campaign, he awaits his lunch without desire. Amid the terrifying whistle of the grenades, he stands straight in the field, calm because he has done what he could to protect his soldiers, while thinking of the arduous trial that growing old has in store for him, after all the disappointment and bitterness of the present. I see that his tie is positioned forever higher on his thin neck, leaving his Adam's apple exposed, as it showed itself to be even dirtier than I had imagined. I listen to some of his intelligent observations which he pronounced with a spray of saliva from his tired mouth, and I move away so as not to feel for him, because a soldier should not experience such emotions. He looks at me while I go off with an expression on his face that asks: are you leaving because I have bothered you?]

Here, despite the control Gadda exercises over his material, the image of the captain returning from battle has a strange quality. First he is viewed, from the perspective of hovering wood larks, as a bizarre scarecrow stuck in the earth: a yellow, malevolent monster who surveys the world with a funereal eye. The lyrical enchantment of the initial image of the peaceful highlands is abruptly interrupted by his presence, which gives rise to the birds' shrill cry of warning. We begin thus with an allegory, an otherness that stands in for the real captain who comes clearly into view at soon as the perspective changes to that of the narrator. The figure of the old captain is now constructed so as to give credence to the apprehension his presence has caused; to do so Gadda accentuates its features by placing that otherness, so to speak, on stage, deforming, however slightly, its realistic presence by means of detailed insistence. What results is a (baroque) excess of the figure; its material presence overwhelms, as the writing, which began on a serene note, becomes emotional. But it is much less compassion that Gadda feels for the doleful figure he creates than irony, self-irony: the captain-scarecrow is an allegory of the author himself, forced to live *in extremis*, awaiting a promotion that will never come. We have therefore in this literary experiment the first in a long line of Gaddian *Doppelgängerin*. By highlighting the grotesqueness of this figure deformed by fate, Gadda conveys his

own personal desperation that derives from the 'ardua prova che il decadere della vita gli serba.' We are at the beginning of Gadda's baroque
expressionism and the modern melancholy which, as Benjamin has
written, derives from self-estrangement.[8]

The scarecrow-captain, frozen in the fields of war, is Gadda's first literary experience of loss. The figure contains in embryo what will
become a distinctive style of the grotesque, the ultimate aims of which
are explicitly pronounced at the outset of *Il castello di Udine*:

Tendo a una brutale deformazione dei temi che il destino s'è creduto di propo-
nermi come formate cose ed obbietti: come paragrafi immoti della sapiente sua
legge. Umiliato dal destino, sacrificato all'inutilità, nella bestialità corrotto, e
però atterrito dalla vanità vana del nulla, io, che di tutti li scrittori dell' Italia
antichi e moderni sono quello che piú possiede di comodini da notte, vorrò
dipartirmi un giorno dalle sfinancate séggiole dove m'ha collocato la sapienza e
la virtú de'sapienti e de'virtuosi, e, andando verso l'orrida solitudine mia, levarò
in lode di quelli quel canto, a che il mandolino dell'anima, ben grattato, potrà
dare bellezza nel ghigno. (*CU*, 119)

[I tend towards a brutal deformation of the themes that destiny has thought to
put forth to me as things and objects already formed: as motionless paragraphs
in her wise law. Humbled by destiny, sacrificed to uselessness, corrupted by the
crudeness around me, and thus terrified by the vacuous vanity of nothingness, I,
who of all the ancient and modern writers of Italy possess the most night tables,
will some day want to lift myself out of the broken-down chairs to which I have
been assigned by the wisdom and the virtue of the wise and virtuous, and, moving towards my horrific solitude, I shall sing in praise of them a song which,
through the well-strummed mandolin of my spirit, will give beauty to my
sneer.]

Il castello di Udine begins on this note of dislocation. Gadda's humanist
assurances have been undermined by a cruel fate; thus history (i.e., his
life-history) has become a personal catastrophe, a time of ruin and exile.
The key word in this passage is 'legge.' The wise law of destiny, articulated within a closed system of philosophical truth, ensures the progress
of reason. The rupture has occurred here in the law and is amplified
throughout the rational systems upholding it. There is Freudian inflection to Gadda's use of the term 'law,' which he makes plain in an accompanying note: 'sistema di inibizioni che costituiscono eredità normativa
della tribù. Nel caso del Ns. la tribù è il ceto mercativo-politecnico di

Milano e dintorni' (system of inhibitions which constitute the normative heredity of the tribe. In our author's case, the tribe is the business-technological class of Milan and surroundings). The law then for Gadda is synonymous with culture. However personalized, Gadda's awareness of the collapse of an ideal nineteenth-century world is not fundamentally different from that expressed much earlier by Leopardi or Nietzsche against the illusions of progress or, in his own time, by a large family of modernist writers for whom modernization sounded the death knell of civilization. It is, moreover, the same baroque awareness of disaster that toppled the ontological security of Renaissance form. Quevedo and Caravaggio are artists particularly dear to Gadda because they, like him, based their work on a principle of dissonance and disillusion. The historical trauma itself, however, although it does not dictate the form of a response, establishes the position from which the subject will respond. The contradiction Gadda describes between himself and the world polarizes two extremes: history as a sovereign force, and the self as the ultimate difference. It does so in such a way that the self, while exhibiting its world of ruins as a means of disenchantment, makes it clear that history's dominance can be challenged by the subject's will to assert itself in the face of disaster, by its will to power. In other words, we are not dealing with the writer's subjection to his negative destiny, his capitulation before history, and thus with the desire to take refuge in reverie, myth, melancholy, or any other transcendental object of pleasure. We are dealing instead with a face-to-face confrontation, enemies paired off against each other, and willing to fight to the very end. If destiny has willed Gadda's horrific solitude, if it has humbled him and made him run with the pack, he will take his revenge. He will devise a language that will at once lay bare reality and speak the idiom of alienation. Like the history that has caused the death of his ideal, the language of vindication, the 'ghigno' (sneer) produced by his 'ben grattato' (well-strummed) mandolin is a destructive principle, the circus mirror of a fragmented world.

'Tendo al mio fine' goes on to list, as variations on the same theme of grotesque representation, the various fragmented objects that will come under the weight of his pen. The identity of these objects, however, is less important for our discussion than the peculiar formal characteristics of the piece in which they appear. There is little Gadda says about the war in the *Giornale di guerra e prigionia* and *Il castello di Udine* that cannot be found in the numerous published diaries, journals, and correspondence of fellow combatants. Instead, the war gains its force by the way it is represented, by its emotional intensity, by its figural quality and the excess of meaning it generates, and by its radicalization of the subject. 'Tendo al mio fine,' in other words, while stating the aims of Gadda's writing, discloses the fundamental attributes of a style: a formal strategy designed precisely to provide the writing subject with a maximum of difference.

A distinctive feature of *Il castello di Udine* is that it comes equipped with Gadda's own commentary, in the form of notes, written by an obviously fictitious Dott. Feo Averrois (word-play on Dante's' 'Averroè che il gran commento feo').[9] The prefatory note, signed by Averrois and fashioned in a language and syntax reminiscent of Manzoni's facetious imitation of his rediscovered seventeenth-century manuscript, is meant as an ironic reflection of the authorial self whose actual writing will often resemble that of his commentator. The notes, however, in an equally ironic counter-move, appear in a scientific, explanatory style, typical of Gadda's essays, and totally devoid of the baroque conceits and syntactical inflections of the prefatory note.

What objective subtends this splitting of the subject? Is it just another tactic attributable to what the commentator calls 'l'ambiguo de' di lui modi e processi' (the ambiguity in his modes and processes)? Why, in other words, is interpretation necessary? The critical language of the notes constitutes another space independent of the subject and its consciousness. Interpretation, as Buci-Glucksmann puts it in her reading of Benjamin, 'grasps an enigmatic (familiar and alien) reality by building a concrete mass of constellations and significations, where meaning is never more than the effect of a machinery which condenses time and reveals it by relating it to the present' (1994: 66–7). That Gadda wants to give the impression that someone else is writing, while at the same time making it amply clear that both narration and interpretation are the work of the same subject, illustrates at once his awareness of the fragmentary character of representation and the essential 'playfulness' of the enterprise called literature. In the case of the book *Il castello di Udine*, Gadda gives notice of his intention to defend his baroque modernity, which, after the publication of *La Madonna dei filosofi*, was already under siege. His means of defence is in itself profoundly baroque: namely, to fragment his self as object, dispersing it into the enigmatic extremes, manifest in the use of different linguistic and stylistic registers. Hence the alienation produced by self-interpretation is doubled by fixing the all-too-familiar reality common to the war literature of his times in a strange new idiom, designed to shock, to disorient, and, most of all, to transform catastrophe into linguistic spectacle.

In *Il castello di Udine*, Gadda is revisiting the war from a distance of more than ten years. The passing of chronological time, however, has increased rather than diminished the alienation. The external chaos of the battlefield and encampments has now become the natural order of the universe. The substance of a lived experience has been transformed into an allegory of loss. The strange and horrific aspects of the author's life nest amid the confusion. The writing self, with its power of analysis, violence, and irony, must confront the chaos:

Leggendo certe pagine del *Principe* non si riesce quasi a capire se sono verità o ferocia o spasimante ironia. Forse i tre termini sono uno solo, fuori dal minestrone dei miti. Navigare nella minestra, ma cercar di capire come è fatta. (*CU*, 130)

[Reading certain pages of *The Prince* it is almost difficult to understand whether they are truth or ferocity or convulsive irony. Perhaps the three terms are one only, beyond the minestrone of myth. Navigate in the soup, but try to find out how it is made.]

The aphoristic tone of this passage underlines its deep moral sense. To suggest that truth, violence, and irony are one and the same is to bring forth a principle of writing, designed to dismantle the manifest truths of reality. Violence and irony, the main ingredients of satire, constitute a means by which a particular form is deformalized and dislocated. Truth does not emerge from this process as an effect of the destruction. Rather it is itself the process, fixed in polysemic imagery, which deforms and destroys:

Tendo a una sozza dipintura della mandra e del suo grandissimo e grossissimo intelletto [...]

Coglierò ghirlande di rose e sentirò musiche di dolcissimi pifferi: e farò veder su nave grandissimi commodori e armirati, e corbe di broccoli: e tutto saravvi [...]

Conterò sogni e chimere, come, sospinta dal vespero, si deforma la rosea nube del cielo: e conterò li sputi e catarri de' contadini nostri e saranno per avventura passati trenta nel quadro d'un piede [...]

Cosi' seguiterò il mio cammino solitario. Seguiterò a pagare e servire la necessità, conterò avaramente il poco denaro, loderò la plastile carne delle infarinate bagasce; appetitirò cose non lecite; altre sognerò non possibili; e una grata sarà il termine dei pochi miei passi. E leggerò i libri sapientissimi degli scrittori, infino a che, sopra la mia trapassata sapienza, vi crescerà l'erba. (*CU*, 120–2)

[I tend to a filthy portrait of the herd and of its enormous, rude intellect ...

I shall gather wreaths of roses and listen to the music of the sweetest of flutes: and I'll portray great commodores and admirals, and baskets of broccoli: and everything will be present ...

I shall recount dreams and chimeras, how, guided by vespers, the rosy cloud is deformed in the sky: and I shall recount the spittle and phlegm of our country folk, thirty specimens of which by chance will have fallen within the quadrant of a foot ...

Thus I shall follow my solitary path. I shall continue to pay and serve necessity, count avariciously the little money, praise the plastic-like skin of made-up whores; I shall desire forbidden things, and dream of others as not possible and my short journey will terminate behind a grate. And I shall read the books of the wisest of writers, until grass grows on the wisdom I have accumulated.]

The combination of dissociation and hysteria in these sentences produces a spectacle in which every tendency to embellish the fragmented self with some lyrical continuity is defeated. It is in this sense that *Il castello di Udine* sets itself apart from the war literature of the times, which tended towards romantic victimization, prompted by the death of a friend or the retreat of Italian troops from a beloved town. The ruins of Gadda's past are here filtered through a perspective of grief and melancholy. Like Baudelaire, whom he cites in a note ('Ma jeunesse ne fut qu'un ténébreux orage' (*CU*, 122, n. 4; My youth was but a dark storm), Gadda's fate, too, is to live in 'disillusion and permanent unreality' (Buci-Glucksmann 1994: 155).

The object of melancholic loss is in *Il castello di Udine* none other than the 'motherland' (*patria*), the symbolic, maternal body for which Gadda went to war. The assembled book, with its labyrinthine contents and continual intersecting of past and present, is a journey across the paradoxes and ambivalences of the war and its aftermath in search of the traces of a ruined civilization. In 'Crociera mediterranea' the impulse towards redemption and fulfilment is stifled by a strong existential anxiety. The aims of a peaceful cruise and the writer's state of mind are incompatible. A Mediterranean vacation provided Gadda with the opportunity to travel back to his cultural origins, 'alla proda della luce e della serenità' (to the border of light and serenity) towards 'il lembo meraviglioso della fecondità' (the marvellous threshold of fecundity). But such a mythical return, rather than being a romantic flight from reality, becomes a destructive principle. The ironic smile of reason ('il sorriso di chi la sa lunga' [the smile of someone who knows the whole story]) is a strong obstacle to any idyllic fusion of mind and emotion in the contemplation of transcendence. The acute consciousness of crisis and catastrophe blocks the natural, lyrical movement of the narrator's being. The past of war, the historical trauma, is fixed in his memory; it is his only point of reference. The style as a result is fragmented in recurrent visual and psychological obsessions; interpolations and flashbacks fill the pages, thus amplifying and complicating the commentary. The past cannot be retained as memory; it appears for a moment, but quickly gives way to violent outbursts and caricature. Gadda has dilated time into the time of war. It is the now which takes precedence in a reality of perpetual antimony.

If there is a common thread holding together the many disparate pieces that comprise *Il castello di Udine*, it is contained in the remark uttered at the beginning of 'Tendo al mio fine': that the law 'ignora o misconosce le ragioni oscure e vivide della vita, la qual devolve profonda' (ignores or misapprehends the obscure and vigorous movement of life that devolves in depth). In discussing Benjamin's concept of the political in baroque theatre, Buci-Glucksmann underlines Benjamin's remark that 'in baroque theater "the sovereign is the representative of history. He holds the course of history in his hand like a sceptre"'(68). She goes on to comment that, for Benjamin, 'the Prince is the Cartesian God transposed to the field of politics' (ibid) and that, for this politics to develop, it must do so in a 'state of emergency,' of crisis or catastrophe. Her point is that, in baroque drama, the 'logic of power encompasses its despotic-worldly reality' and that 'the truth of history lies no longer on the side of the law, norm or regulation,' but rather 'in the violence of a sovereign, which asserts itself to the extreme in states of emergency'(69). Benjamin's argument has a special relevance for our discussion of the logic underlying Gadda's modern baroque perspective, and particularly, as we shall see, for an understanding of how the pieces of *Il castello di Udine* fit together.

In war, reason has relinquished its truth to catastrophe, history becoming one with violence and the irrational. Unlike in the seventeenth century, in the twentieth there is no sovereign to dictate and combat violence with violence, thus there is no 'vicious circle of the political, where absolute power rises up on the basis of catastrophes, in order to avert catastrophe'(ibid). Hence there is no basis for the baroque tragedy of a Shakespeare or a Calderon. Without the Prince as an objective political force, the conditions of the historical baroque drama are missing. The liberal state, with its regard for the masses, not only has forfeited despotism (therefore the potential for tragedy it contained), but, as a result, has joined the high with the low, the tragic with the comic. The objective space of the sovereign is transformed into a different site of emergency, one now governed by a perspective that is thoroughly subjective, by the one in the many, a perspective that, given the object-world of difference, is forced to combine truth, violence, and satire. It is thus that we understand Gadda's aphoristic remark about Machiavelli: 'Leggendo certe pagine del Principe non si riesce quasi a capire se sono verità o ferocia o spasimante ironia. Forse i tre termini sono uno solo, fuori dal ministrone dei miti. Navigare nella minestra, ma cercar di capire come è fatta'(*CU*, 130). The 'minestra,' for Gadda, is in fact a 'minestrone': a world of innumerable fragments, which, at first glance, would appear horrifically undecipherable. But it is the 'second glance' that concerns us. If there is truth in violence, it is generated by the violence of satire ('spasimante ironia'). It is now not the power of the sovereign that – paradoxically (according to Benjamin) – initiates the breakdown of the rational, but rather the false sovereign of the democratic idea which in Gadda's particular case translates into what he regards as unbridled individualism and disrespect for authority. But just as the Prince's omnipotence can develop only on the 'ground of catastrophe,' so it is with Gadda that order can be restored only through the assertion of the self and the total disregard for the law: to lay bare reality, strip it naked, remake it into a language of a world that has been shattered into fragments.

The baroque excess of meaning in Gadda is not intended as a means of probing the complexity of the world of phenomena; nor is it Gadda's purpose in his descriptions of things and perceptions to reveal some objective governing principle, to capture, in the vein of Manzoni, a logic that governs human affairs. The signifier in Gadda is of the allegorical kind discussed by Benjamin in *The Origin of German Tragic Drama*: 'it does not achieve transcendence by being voiced,' rather it remains 'self-sufficient and intent on the display of it own substance' (201). The 'bombast' of baroque drama, he goes on to say, provides its own justification 'as a consistently purposeful and constructive linguistic gesture'(ibid). Benjamin is, of course, counterpoising the written and spoken languages of drama ('word-baroque' and 'image-baroque'), his point being that the 'division between written language and intoxicating spoken language opens up a gulf in the solid massif of verbal meaning and forces the gaze into the depths of language' (ibid). In Gadda, the rift between materiality and meaning is plain in the more polemical and his-

trionic moments of his writing, when the power of emotion sets off a linguistic chain reaction, as in 'Tendo al mio fine' and some of the excerpts
from the *Giornale* cited above. These are moments when the writing
becomes a spectacle, and the objects described lose any inherent meaning they might have had, to become, as Benjamin puts it 'the ecstasy of
the creature [...]exposure, rashness, powerlessness before God'(ibid).
Although Gadda's spectacle results from a powerlessness before the
world, like in the *Trauerspiel* discussed by Benjamin, it is an attempt to
break free from conventional meaning and thus assert the power inherent in the prisoner.

History, Gadda states more than once, has conspired against him; the
world is intrigue and he, like Gonzalo in *La cognizione*, is forced to give
himself over to the power of things. Hence it is possible to establish a
psychological frame that holds in place the fragments that comprise *Il
castello di Udine* and to show how the experience of war and imprisonment become, for Gadda, a literary trope. We referred above to the gulf
between the ideal and the real in Gadda's war experience. These anti-
thetical moments crystallize in two different modes of expression typical of *Il castello di Udine*, one lyrical and symbolic, the other, historical
and allegorical. (I am using 'symbolic' and 'allegorical' in Benjamin's
sense of the terms.) The lyrical, symbolic moment is a single, instanta-
neous moment in time: the present time of memory that does not
endure, a parenthesis in the flow of events in which meaning is wholly
present and complete. By contrast, allegory is a return to historical time,
to the reality of disconnected things; it registers the subject's movement
in the world and in time in search of meaning; it is history in all of its
horrors and pain. In Gadda's narratives, these two moments intersect
or are juxtaposed, which results in the displacement of meaning and
the distortion or corruption of the image. A useful illustration of this
process can be found in 'Sibili dentro le valli,' the third part of 'Polem-
iche e pace nel direttissimo,' and the piece that stands as the *Explicit*
to *Il castello di Udine* and, therefore, in direct relation to 'Tendo al
mio fine.'

The scene in 'Sibili' is a train journey from Rome to Milan. For the
young Gadda, whose professional responsibilities necessitated frequent
travelling, the train was a stage across which passed a large variety of
people, the space of a comic pageant which he saw as history and
recounted as chronicle. Before this collection of human objects, the narrator places himself not in the posture of an objective viewer, but rather
as someone forced to endure. The reader perceives immediately the split

between the self and history, between an ideal of harmony and the reality of chaos and fragmentation. For the self, the world is wrapped in melancholy: 'Dai monti dell'Umbria il vento notturno buttava l'acqua diaccia a gocciolare contro la luce dei cristalli. Teróntola risuonò fiocamente, nel croscio solitario della pioggia, senza sigari sigarette, senza nessuno'(265; From the mountains of Umbria the night wind hurled drops of cold rain against the lighted windows. Teróntola resounded meekly, in the solitary rattle of the rain, without cigars cigarettes, without anyone). This initial paragraph is significant because it contains the alteration of focus typical of the Gaddian baroque. The melancholic voice does not persist in the lyrical mode, which, if it did, would produce a more sustained funereal tone of decadence. Instead, the echoes of D'Annunzian syntax ('risuonò fiocamente,''croscio solitario') are destabilized by the intrusion of history ('senza sigari sigarette') and, as the narration progresses, the melancholic traveller, entranced by the flashes of landscape and the monotonous sound of the rain beating against the windows of the speeding train, becomes a chronicler of the everyday, mundane spectacle of life. The transition from symbol to allegory is embodied in the perception of a figure who enters the compartment in which the narrator is seated: a 'signore ammantellato e nero' (a dark figure in a cape), who for a moment appears as 'il fuggente cavaliere dello Heine' (Heine's fleeing horseman), an image which sparks the author's memory of the poet's solitary, melancholic soldier: 'Il vento dell'autunno scuote gli alberi – La notte è umida e fredda – Ravvolto nel mio cupo mantello – Cavalco, solo, traverso foresta ...' (265; The autumn wind beats against the trees – The night is cold and damp – Wrapped in my dark cape – Alone, I ride across the forest ...), which he glosses in a note with the original verses: 'Gehült im grauen Mantel – Reite ich einsam im Wald' (280). But just as in the *Giornale,* where the figure of the scarecrow in the field becomes the desperate captain, the lyrical image of the soldier cloaked in his dark cape is restored to history: 'Ma si trattava di un maresciallo pilota, i di cui cinque sensi si appalesarono magistralmente collaudati al Laboratorio Psicofisico Centrale della R. Aeronautica, tanta fu la prontezza e la energia con cui volle richiudere' (265; But it was only a pilot major whose five senses appeared magisterially tested at the Central Psychophysical Laboratory of the Royal Air Force, such was the quickness and the energy with which he wanted to close the door.) At this point in the narration, the world of the solitary, melancholic subject at the centre of *Il castello di Udine,* that baroque landscape of ruins that sparks the subject's spontaneous, lyrical escape into the symbolic, is shattered into fragments, as the narrator becomes hyper-conscious of the multiple conversations and utterings that fill the claustrophobic space of the compartment, of the aimless chatter, of all the pieces and emblems of common existence that he will now transform slowly into spectacle:

In sincronismo con le battute di rotaia, le gioviali traiettorie del suo collo [of the 'l'uomo senza scarpe, tutto in ascolto' whom, one can assume, is Gadda himself] ad elevata periodicità porgevano grandissime orecchie incontro alla catarsi ed al ritmo, alla pagina quintessenziata e all'umanità dei personaggi, alla scrittura e alla dialettica, 'a tutto un mondo' vivente in Rostòff e agli 'onanismi calligrafici', invece, di Pinco Ponza; grandissimi orecchioni incontro alla virgoletta, alla paroletta, al singhiozzo, al suono, al tono, al colore, al sapore. Poi arrivarono anche la linfa, la vita, il pàlpito, e di nuovo l'estetica; poi l'etica occidentale, il Cristianesimo, l'arte, i coglioni duri, il barocco, il romanzo, la lirica, il film. Agli eroi retorici e classicheggianti del vacuo Bertoloni venne contrapposta la figura meravigliosamente complessa della Caterina Vistolòwna Vigolaiewnska, istitutrice sadica all'orfano epilettico e tubercolotico Ciùchin (oh! Quella scena della mano nei pantaloni!): personaggio estremamente riuscito anche lui, radiato ventitreenne dalle file dell'esercito come alcoolòmane e ubriacone abituale, morto poi di dissenteria presso Nishnij-Novgorod, contrariamente al consueto de'bevitori, che in Italia hanno degli intestini di ferro [...]
Ràpidi sullo schermo timpànico, travolti da spira di bufera, passano in quelle voci Valmichi ed Achille, Menelao becco e la non-esistenza di Omero: le sette città natali di costui e la tragedia sofoclea, la nèmesi e il fato, la Grazia e il libero arbitrio, i primitivi senesi e Ada Negri, la Giovane Parca e i capponi di Renzo, la Commedia Umana e il Tempo Perduto; senza contare i Karamazoff, i Rougon-Maquart, i Vela, i Nibelunghi, i Malavoglia, i Bencivenga; e l'autobiografia di Garibaldi. (CU, 267–8)

[In synchrony with the thumping sound of the rails, the jovial movement of his neck in heightened response harmonized with the catharsis and the rhythm, with the quintessentialized page and the humanity of the characters, with writing and dialectics, with 'a whole world' living in Rostòff and, instead, with the 'calligraphic masturbation' of Pinco Ponza; the biggest of big ears attentive to the comma, word, sigh, sound, tone, colour, taste. Then even the lymph, life, palpitation, and again aesthetics; then Western ethics, Christianity, art, hard balls, the baroque, the novel, poetry, film. Juxtaposed to the classic rhetorical heros of vacuous Bertoloni was the marvellously complex figure of Caterina Vis-

tolowna Vigolaiewnska, the sadistic nurse of the epileptic and tuberculous
Ciùchin (oh! That scene with his hand in his pants!): he too a very successful
character, radiant twenty-three- year-old fresh from the army, a habitual drunk,
who died of dissentry near Nishnij-Novgorod, in contrast to the usual drinkers,
who in Italy have iron stomachs …

   Rapidly on to the tympanic screen, often like sharp gusts, Valmichi and Achil-
les, Menelaus and the non-existence of Homer pass through those voices: the
seven cities of his birth and Sophoclean tragedy, nemesis and the fates, Grace
and free will, the Sienese primitives and Ada Negri, the Young Fate and Renzo's
capons, the Comédie Humaine and La Recherche; without counting the Karam-
azovs, the Rougon-Maquarts, the Velas, the Nibelungs, the Malavoglias, the
Bencivengas; and the autobiography of Garibaldi.]

These are just two samples of chaotic listings, inventories of vacuous
discourse, in themselves lifeless, but re-formed by the now hysterical
subject into a grotesquely comic procession. The materials that Gadda
parades before the reader's mind, this limitless kalideoscope of signification, has but one single purpose: to disorient and, ultimately, to dis-
place the reader. Gadda, the melancholic subject of this narrative, whose
primary intent is to affirm his subjectivity by means of asserting total
control over his representation, produces an excess of signification that
undermines his position and, with it, his desire to control and safeguard
his wounded self. The more the narrator extends his parade of images,
the more he endeavours to exhaust the expressive potential of the contents of the *direttissimo* and the landscapes it traverses, the more he himself is caught in the labyrinth of his own making, that is, within a
language that can never fix meaning in a sense that it embraces the
entire narrative and, thus, provides the reader with a focus. This play of
signs defeats representation, as the narrator, while he remains on the
register of history, is forced to include his own self among the infinite
list of things he has deconstructed: 'le due calze dell'ingegnere, con dentro i due piedi, sdrusciavano semisecche sopra il linòleum, mentre le
scarpe andarono subitamente a remengo fra i piedi di tutti' (270–1; The
engineer's two socks, inside of which his two feet, somewhat dryly
rubbed on the linoleum, while his shoes quickly scattered among everyone's feet). His only recourse is to return to melancholy, and from there
to spiral back to some possible (absent) cause of his impotency that the
writing has supplanted. He does so by making the comic play of signs
abruptly open out onto drama. The body of a young man ('vestito da
ciclista, d'un ciclismo di pochissima spesa'[271; dressed like a cyclist,

but poorly]) is carried into the compartment. He had gotten off the train at Teróntola and jumped back on to the baggage car while the train was in motion; when he leaned out to close the door, his head was crushed between the door and the loading gauge. His name, we learn, was Carlo Rusconi; he left a poor, widowed mother and a girlfriend (Clotilde Ramazzotti Lonate Boffalora). The lifeless body is now the focus of the narrative. The object exhibited is a totalizing presence, but always on the verge of being fragmented into the perspectives of the onlookers. But unlike other lifeless, or dead, bodies we find in Gadda's works, this corpse retains a certain dignity of composure in spite of the confusion of the onlookers and the train's sudden jolts. The body signals a space of absence, of loss, that can be filled only with melancholy, the subject's principal vehicle of lack, which at once protects and exposes the autobiographical voice:

Verde Lombardia! Dove di già è scesa la bruma, le desolate nevi! La cucchiara vi si dimanda cazzuola, e il mattone quadrello. Il pane di Como non è da tutti; bisogna girare, andare! Costruire le chiese a Dàndolo, a Sermoneta le case.

Gli impiccati hanno avuto una tomba; ma i morti di fame dove andranno a sbattere? Il grembo della mamma non può riprenderli indietro.

Le bielle tramutavano in disperata corsa l'impulso; con sibili dentro le buie valli il direttissimo strascinava ogniduno al suo caso; la polemica della cucchiara era stata più dura dell'altra. E ognuno, dopo la rissa, voleva rabbracciare la mamma. Forse i tre pezzi bastavano! ... Con i calzoni frusti, con il portafogli ragnato ... Oh! La cucina era fredda, senza più rame né voci, offuscati contro il camino Podgòra e Mrzli, e l'artigliere chino verso le ombre al traino, come al Calvario ... Oh! Ma la mamma! (*CU*, 274)

[Green Lombardy! Where the mist and desolate snow had just fallen. The bucket seeks its trowel and the brick its tile. The bread of Como is not for everyone. You have to move about, go! Build churches in Dandolo, houses in Serroneta.

The hanged want a gravestone: but the hungry where do they end up? Their mothers' wombs cannot take them back.

The connecting rods transmuted the impulse desperately; with the hissing of the wind in the dark valleys the train dragged everyone to their fate; the argument about the bucket was more fierce than the other. And everyone, after the riot, wanted to hug his mother. Perhaps the three pieces were enough! ... With worn-out pants and threadbare wallet ... Oh! the kitchen was cold, without either copper or voices, Podgòra and Mrzli obscure against the trail and the gunner bent over in the shadows of his truck, as at Calvary ... Oh! But Mamma!]

As the corpse, made steady by the compassionate gesture of the soldier, surrenders itself to the subject's melancholic gaze, we are transported into another text, into a store of desperate images that revert to the auto-biographical soul of the writing. We have already crossed the boundary into *La cognizione del dolore*.

3

Creative Bodies: Theory and Practice of the Grotesque

Italian prose fiction in the early twentieth century, like the modernist currents in the rest of Europe, was characterized by its belief in the novel as an ideal vehicle for the exploration of individual subjectivity. The conception of the self that informed the works of all the major writers of the period, however different its modes of identification and transmission, placed the human subject (the protagonist as embodiment of the consciousness of the author) at centre stage, where it was made to command constant attention. There it bore the burden of being represented as a subject 'in crisis' in order to reconstitute itself in and through the very experience that challenged its integrity. Through the representation of an afflicted or disquieted subjectivity, the fulfilment denied to the subject at the level of theme was achieved at the formal level, its status decided by a language and a style that belonged to it alone and that qualified it as the central agent of the narrative act. To put it differently, the individual subject in the principal narrative texts of Italian modernism, from D'Annunzio to Pirandello and Svevo, was always the subject of representation, which, to use Heidegger's phrasing, is the place where the truth of the world speaks itself. And it was by narrating itself that the subject 'in crisis' gained the reassuring certainty of myth.

The main lines of Gadda's development that converge in his baroque manner all intersect at one principal (aesthetic and ethical) concern: to extract the self from representation by making its existence as a narrative structure problematic. This will entail the work of petrification, a virtual killing of the self, making the self thing-like by reducing it to a grotesque surface reality. The theoretical basis for such a procedure is to a notable degree already present in *Meditazione milanese*, the work in which Gadda establishes his philosophical interest in the interrelation of the self, consciousness, and the object world of perception.

Meditazione milanese begins with a disclaimer: that the philosopher's terrain is unstable ('Il terreno del filosofo è la mobile duna o la savana deglutitrice'[1] [The philosopher's terrain is the mobile sand dune or the ingesting savana.]) and, moreover, that the author's particular journey of knowledge has no star to guide it. At the same time, his faith in the mind's ability to disentangle reality gives him confidence to venture on. Gadda, who had studied Kantian philosophy with Piero Martinetti in Milan,[2] maintained that order in the universe was possible because the conscious mind was capable of perceiving it. However, this starting point did not presuppose for him (as it did for Kant) that consciousness was an unalterable, *a priori* given.[3] Instead, he believed that states of consciousness were variable and thus capable of changing with every new perception. Gadda's approach to knowledge is, in Giano Carlo Roscioni's words, 'constructivist,'[4] which means that every moment or phase in the acquisition of knowledge is perceived as a system in itself. So even if Gadda remained confident in the mind's capacity to order the world, he sensed early on that human expression was not always governed by the conscious mind. And while it is right to maintain, as Roscioni does, that everything in Gadda's philosophical repertoire seems to be under the control of his pragmatic spirit, common sense, and preference for exact, concrete analyses, it cannot be ignored that his fundamental notions about reality run counter to his stated belief that the multiple data of the universe can be ordered into ready-made concepts.

In any case, however problematic Gadda's relationship with philosophy might have been, it was a lasting relationship that helped sharpen his interest in psychoanalysis and that extended to the heart of his fiction. It is no coincidence that 'L'egoista,' a dialogue on self-love written in 1953, echoes notions from *Meditazione* on multiplicity and dialectical causality that are part and parcel of Detective Ingravallo's oft-cited philosophical wisdom: 'Sosteneva, fra l'altro, che le inopinate catastrofi non sono mai la conseguenza o l'effetto che dir si voglia d'un unico motivo, d'una causa al singolare: ma sono come un vortice, un punto di depressione ciclonica nella coscienza del mondo, verso cui hanno cospirato tutta una molteplicità di causali convergenti' (QP, 17; He sustained, among other things, that unforeseen catastrophes are never the consequence or the effect, if you prefer, of a single motive, of *a* cause singular; but they are rather like a vortex, a cyclonic point of depression in the consciousness of the world, towards which a whole multitude of converging causes have contributed [*AM*, 5]). Ingravallo's 'philosophy' no doubt regulates the universe of Gaddian narrative, which, like a 'vortex' or 'cyclonic point of depression,' is made up of constant alteration (deformation), disturbances, and changes of tension and energy.[5]

There are two sides to this vision present in *Meditazione*. One is characteristically Leibnizian, rooted in the conviction that the universe is correlated to the extent that an event occurring in any of its parts has a recoiling or rebounding effect in all of the others. As Gadda has Teofilo state at the beginning of 'L'egoista': 'Se una libellula vola a Tokyo, innesta una serie di reazioni che raggiungono me' (*VM*, 654; If a dragonfly flies in Tokyo, it initiates a series of reactions that reach me.) Gadda also takes from Leibniz his idea of the monad: multiple, self-enclosed, autonomous centres of force of which the universe is made. And it would not be an exaggeration to say that the multilingualism and polyphony[6] so characteristic of Gadda's writings finds one of their many lines of support in Leibniz's notion of 'possible worlds' which are not far in kind from the 'plurality of worlds' described in modern physics. But Gadda's Leibniz has been filtered through rather extensive readings of Bergson. And it is this side of Gadda's intellectual formation that is decisive.

Meditazione milanese is a philosophical reflection on knowledge. Its principal argument may be summarized as follows. If it is true that knowledge presupposes the organization of a particular datum in a system, it is also true that the configuration of that system depends on the predisposition of the knowing subject: 'La nostra analisi [riceve] inizio da un nostro dato psicologico e storico, cioè personale ed ambientale, che si devolve in un flusso, che è in una velocità; che è labile, mobile'[7] (Our analysis begins from a psychological or historical datum, personal and environmental, that devolves in a flux, rapid movement; it is open to change, mobile). Here the adjectives 'storico,' 'personale,' and 'ambientale' collapse into 'psicologico.' Knowledge is a psychological experience of the subject who changes (alters or deforms) the datum by inserting into it his perception of it. Knowledge for Gadda is thus a *becoming* in the Bergsonian sense of *duration*, that is, a continuous enlarging of experience; simply stated, a process. As the object of knowledge, the datum itself exists in flux; we intuit it as a system, but it is a system existing in relation to other systems. The datum, however, does not exist in a state of pure becoming. While our perception of it deforms its previous composition, something remains or 'persists': a trace of what was. Here too Gadda seems to have drawn from Bergson's ideas on change and substance, maintaining, as he does, the continuation in existence of some sort of substrate. For it would be impossible to make sense of a universe in which change is not the change of something: 'Se tutto fosse movibile e mosso, nessuna forma o figura sarebbe pensata' (631; If everything was movable or moved, it would be impossible to think of any form or figure). But the substrate cannot escape having been affected by the change it experiences. Therefore what continues in an imperfect state, influenced by the change in its surrounding components, Gadda takes as an example the game of chess.[8] The configuration of the pieces on the chessboard constitutes a system. The movement of any one piece in the original configuration introduces a change into the system which deforms it in the sense that it bears upon all subsequent moves. The deforming element is one single piece that, in its having been moved, acts on the remaining elements of the system. While they continue to exist as a system, their existence, on account of the original deformation, is flawed. ('L'elemento deformatore sembra a noi essere il solo pezzo attualmente mosso, mentre la restante massa dei pezzi ci appare il "persistere attuale" del sistema: è peraltro un persistere sui generis, un persistere che risente della mossa eseguita, un gramo e imperfetto persistere altro' [631; The deforming element appears to us as the only piece that has actually been moved, while all the other pieces appear as what 'persists' of the system: it is moreover a *sui generis* persistence, a persistence that is affected by the move that has been made, a meager and imperfect persistence]). Knowledge then for Gadda is not the re-production in the mind of a reality external to the knower; it is instead a transformative action that consists not in the apprehension of, but in the construction of, meaning:

Data una realtà (sia pure concepita come esterna) l'attribuirle successivamente con penetrante intuito significati integranti, e cioè passare dal significato n-1 ad n, n+1, n+2, è *costruire* perciocché è inserire quella realtà in una cerchia sempre più vasta di relazioni, è un crearla e ricrearla, un formarla e riformarla. (753)

[Attribute to a given reality (even if conceived as external) with penetrating intuition an internal meaning, that is, move from meaning n-1 to n, n+1, n+2, is to *construct* that reality, because it requires that the reality be inserted in an ever wider circle of relations; it is a form of creation and re-creation, a formation and re-formation.]

The construction of meaning by 'knowing' the data of the world is the principal concept of Gaddian epistemology, and it is the idea on which the notion of plurality rests. For when we know, we modify, thus we disturb, realigning, albeit temporarily, the components of a system, changing the tensions and deployment of energy within that system, creating new rhythms in an endless field of becoming. When Gadda attributes to Ingravallo the conviction that cause and effect are never to be considered in the singular, and that entanglement is infinite, he is drawing from the centre of Bergson's philosophy of the real as *élan vital*. The *groviglio* is the essence of life: infinite differentiation and dissociation. Things within the tangle are alienated from their own material form at the very moment they are known, that is, given to the consciousness of others, which initiates the flow of differentiation: 'Nel mondo delle relazioni non esistono monete tesaurizzate nell'arca e dimenticate dalla pulsazione vitale, ma tutte si muovono e rappresentano soltanto rapporti' (649; In the world of relations, there are no coins stored in the mint and forgotten by the vital pulsation of forces; rather they all are in movement and represent only relationships). Thus Gadda makes no attempt to mend the rift he sees between being and meaning. The world is knowable only through the pulsations of the human subject who can make no claim to centrality. And, while Gadda would maintain that the world is to be grasped in relation to the knowing subject as a correlate of its consciousness, unlike the phenomenologists he does not uphold the transcendental nature of that consciousness and, therefore, of subjectivity. The subject is just a part of the world; it has no central position from which it can claim cognitive authority.

The difficulties Gadda encounters in his first attempt at narrating in the classical manner stem directly from his belief that the world of data to which the subject belongs is unstable and that it therefore cannot be represented objectively in its actual parts, for those parts are not separate substances existing in relation to one another and signifying the reality of the whole. But rather, in their *duration,* the parts contract and expand, going beyond their own material limits to constitute a kind of perpetual otherness. In one of the more important 'compositional notes' of *Racconto italiano di ignoto del Novecento*,[9] Gadda remarks that his greatest difficulty in narrating is plot construction; it is crucial that the plot of his novel be not a mere development of a series of events, but that it respond to 'l'istinto delle combinazioni' (instinctual *combinatoire*), the instinct that is 'il profondo ed oscuro dissociarsi della realtà in elementi' (*RI*, 460; The profound and obscure disassociation of reality into elements). In contrast to the 'vecchi romanzi' (old novels), the whole in

Gadda's view is never given, because plots are actual life, and in 'life' there are as many worlds as there are living beings ('quale ingarbugliato intreccio!' [what an entangled plot!]).

Another difficulty for the young Gadda consists in selecting a point of view: 'il punto di vista "organizzatore" della rappresentazione complessa' (the organizational point of view of the complex representation). On this issue, Gadda's notes make a good case for reading him in the light provided by the experimentalists of the Gruppo 63 and which now goes under the sign of textuality or postmodernism. This fundamental narrative category (i.e., 'point of view') grew out of the need in the late nineteenth century to institutionalize the fiction of the individual (bourgeois) subject which was suffering the effects of disintegration and reification in a market economy. It is the instrument that restores form to a consciousness shattered into numerous fragments. While Gadda is aware that representation has as its object the radical plurality of the world that defies systemization or closure, he is concerned with finding a theoretical justification for style. Expression, he states, must be commensurate with point of view, and point of view depends on subjective disposition: 'lo stile mi è imposto dalla passione (intuizione) del momento e [...] lo scrivere con uno stile pre-voluto è uno sforzo bestiale, se questo non è uno stile corrispondente al "mio momento conoscitivo" ' (RI, 461; Style is imposed by the passion (intuition) of the moment and ... writing with a preordained style is an enormous effort, if it is not a style that corresponds to "my cognitive moment"). The problem, Gadda goes on to acknowledge, is that, if he were to write according to the passion of the moment, and therefore employ different points of view and, as a result, different styles, according to subjective disposition, he would be accused of 'variabilità, eterogeneità, mancanza di fusione, mancanza di armonia, et similia' (ibid; variability, heterogeneity, lack of coherence, lack of harmony, etc.), that is, of those very traits that distinguish his work and give it the character of random narration, free association, and unlimited textuality.

In Meditazione milanese, Gadda includes the self in the 'flusso deformatore dell'universo' (deforming flux of the universe [MM, 760]) and makes it clear that his metaphysics prevents him from conceiving of the individual as a unity:

Ogni pausa espressiva è un io e ogni io è una pausa espressiva. Ogni limitazione o allontanamento di relazioni menoma l'io, ogni convergere conferisce all'io, al sistema. E il sistema è una deformazione perenne, che mai non è identico a sé stesso, se non nella grossa apparenza ... (ibid)

[Every expressive pause is an 'I' and every 'I' is an expressive pause. Every limitation or distancing of relations forgets the 'I'',' every convergence confers something to the 'I,' to the system. And the system is a perennial deformation, never identical to itself, save in its outward appearance.]

Hence the self defies individuation and, like the multiplicities that form the world, obeys a logic of its own. Such a position will no doubt affect Gadda's approach to psychoanalysis, as Guido Lucchini has argued, for it is not limited to the areas of metaphysics and poetics but extends also to the sphere of ethics: 'individuation is not only an illusive process, it is an intrinsically evil one' (Lucchini 1997: 177). We shall return to this point later; now it will be useful to consider further the implications that Gadda's anti-substantialist, largely Bergson-inspired, views have for narration.

In Italy, the fiction of the individual subject had already been illustrated by Pirandello, who created an entire aesthetic around the notions of psychic fragmentation and depersonalization. But while Pirandello's narratives and plays disclose all the negative effects of reification, the vision they convey is one in which one's many individual selves coexist, either adapting to the reality they claim to repudiate or exiting from it into myth or madness; the result being that, in defending against fragmentation, Pirandello, like other genuine modernists, forges a powerful ideological instrument: a conception of the world centred on the self. The centre-staging of the self is a means of reinforcing and perpetuating the myth of a world that because of modern science and democracy has disintegrated into self-sufficient fragments. It involves the acceptance of individuation and individual autonomy at the very same time it underscores the relativity of being. It is in this sense that the Pirandellian point of view can be seen as an *a priori* philosophical construct, expressed in a variety of tones but in essentially the same voice. The voice is that of the author, to whom the market economy has given a secondary role to play and to whom Pirandello harks back with nostalgia. It is the subject of narrative, the perspective from which the art work is organized and expressed, that his work, in the last analysis, safeguards.

It becomes clear from the *Racconto* that Gadda's narrative difficulties lie in his inability to find a centre, a stable point of view from which the real can be represented. From his very first entry, we sense Gadda's need to order the chaos within himself; it is from there that the characters and events of his novel must emerge: 'Dal caos dello sfondo devono coagulare e formarsi alcune figure a cui sarà affidata la gestione della favola' (*RI*, 395; From the deep, internal chaos the figures to whom the story will be entrusted must gel and take form). The subject's internal chaos will not lead him to seek order in art regardless of his desire to work out a theoretical dimension in which it is possible to do so. The self in its chaos cannot be internally stabilized, nor can it be fixed in its relation to set boundaries and objects. In other words, its space cannot be circumscribed because it, like the object worlds of its mimetic desires, is trapped in the flux of existence. Therefore, right from the start, Gadda's vision precludes conceiving the novel as the organic reconstruction of character and the social order; it rules out all sorts of historical narratives that depend on history as a repository of truth; and is wary about the liabilities involved in safeguarding the contents of consciousness.

But one must be careful in attributing too much Bergsonism to Gadda. True that his lyric register facilitates the plunge into 'the stream of life' and emotional identification; but the immersion is always temporary and has all the earmarks of a sudden impulse rather than a total vision. The Gaddian self is never lost in fluidity or spontaneity, because it is watched over by an intelligence which checks the compensatory impulse by moving the focus from the private depths of the pure present to the grotesque surface of public reality. Put differently, in Gadda the pain of existence leads not to self-indulgence, but rather to satirical excess. That part of the Gaddian psyche which continually seeks fulfilment in the romantic language of the soul takes on the status of a mere 'text' or 'discourse' subject to revision, commentary, and interpretation. This process is well illustrated in 'Approdo alle Zàttere,' one of the sketches of 'Crociera mediterranea,' contained in *Il Castello di Udine*. Cruising along the coast of Corfu, the traveller (Gadda) reflects on the beauty of the island's capital, pointing to the familiarity of its architecture:

E, in città, case che paiono nostre, come d'un Veneto ottocentesco e pedrocchiano, con presagio di acquate, pieno di estrema poesia: al limite d'un disperato abbandono. Il Foscolo. Poi, se non fosse stata la luce, a una scogliera coronata di cipressi, l'Isola dei Morti, di Böcklin. Ma, poi, il romantico mi parve troppo zelante, m'ero troppo incantato alla sua isola, ai suoi cipressi, alla sua morte. Allora, nel grottesco de'miei dispiaceri vani, dopo la deformazione, il suo significato: l'Isola dei Morti, di De Chirico. (*CU*, 207)

[And, in the city, houses that seems like ours, as in a nineteenth-century, Pedrocchian Veneto, with a foreboding of rain, full of extreme poetry, at the limits of a desperate abandonment. Foscolo. Then, had there not been the light, sea rocks crowned by cypresses, Böcklin's Island of the Dead. But, then, the romantic seemed too zealous, I was too enchanted by his island, by his cypresses, by his death. So then, in the grotesque of my vain displeasures, after the deformation, its meaning: De Chirico's Island of the Dead.]

This commentary on a lived memory describes to a large extent the cognitive process of Gadda's aesthetic. The traveller's gaze falls first on the neoclassical architecture of the city's houses: his response is emotional and driven by an initial impulse towards harmony, but at the same time laced with dread and poetic surrender. Foscolo comes to Gadda's mind: his *I Sepolcri* and *Le Grazie* record the striving of the poet's soul to find an eternal language of 'death' and 'beauty,' as compensation for an existence fragmented by history. Gadda's attention then turns to the cliff, surrounded by cypresses, from which the Swiss painter Arnold Böcklin took inspiration for his *Island of the Dead*. The traveller revisualizes the beauty of Böcklin's dark, melancholic canvas, but immediately realizes the liability of such an escape into a metaphysics of death. The painter's excessive zeal unsettles Gadda's intellect, as he remembers De Chirico's parodic deformation of Böcklin's romantic, supernatural mood.[10] Deformation, he states, generates meaning.

Equally important is the note Gadda appends to this passage, which connects Böcklin's work to the doleful, but heroic, mood of 'l'isola de'poeti' in Carducci's poem 'Presso l'urna di P.B. Shelley.' But crucial to a thorough understanding of the narrator's memory and reflection on it is his gloss of the phrase 'Nel grottesco de' miei dispiaceri vani': 'il suo [the traveller/narrator's] stato d'animo non è da crociera: e risulta di un pasticcio psichico' (his state of mind is not suitable to a cruise: it results from a psychic pastiche), where 'risulta di' indicates not consequence, but rather causality: his state of mind refracts into a psychological tangle: 'Nievo-Ortis-Bandiera bianca-Dalmazia-Corfù' (*CU*, 217). Gadda's position in the cited passage is one of scepticism before the discursive truth of romanticism: De Chirico, in parodying the painting of his former mentor, interrogates its truth claims. But for Gadda the basis of the interrogation lies in an ultimately unrepresentable (because themselves subject to parody) 'dispiaceri vani': not 'worthless pleasures,' it should be noted, but 'worthless sufferings,' ('dispiaceri') which, on account of Gadda's intellectual surveillance, cannot be transformed romantically into art, no matter how tempting the desire. The lyrical-romantic impulse therefore becomes of necessity a register of citations, one among the many elements of pastiche.

The mention of De Chirico, moreover, helps us understand better the function of Gadda's own particular kind of grotesque. The sharp lines and smooth geometrical surfaces that the painter imposes on organic life, his mixing of historically incompatible objects (ancient sculptures and common modern tools, Renaissance buildings and factory smoke-stacks) pose, as do Gadda's own grotesques, an enormous challenge to the Western cultural heritage. A simple example of how Gadda achieves alienation through distortion, reproducing in writing the merciless light that bathes De Chirico's elongated shadows, is his description, in *La cognizione del dolore*, of Battistina, one of the Pirobutirro's domestics, who, descending the path from the villa, runs into the doctor on his way to visit Gonzalo. Like many of Gadda's descriptions, this grotesque portrait of the washerwoman contains a distinct meta-literary directive:

La donna aveva un piccolo incarto sotto il braccio diritto, e con le due mani reggeva un piatto fondo, coperto da un piatto rovesciato: la faccia si rivolgeva a sinistra, che pare si fossero sbagliati a inchiodargliela sul busto, quasi di un pupazzo dignitoso verso occidente: in realtà per far luogo al gozzo, tre o quattro ettogrammi. Aveva l'aria un poco sospettosa e intimidita, con quel desinare che le impegnava le mani, come un animale a cui possano contendere il cibo; e il gozzo pareva un animale per conto suo che, dopo averla azzannata nella trachea, le bevesse fuori metà del respiro, nascondendosi però sotto la pelle di lei come il fotografo sotto la tela. (*CD*, 609)

[The woman had a little package under her right arm, and with both hands she was holding a deep dish, covered by another dish, overturned; her face was addressed to the left, so it seemed that they had been mistaken when they fastened it to her bust, like a dignified puppet facing west – in reality, to make room for her goiter, three or four hectograms. Her manner was a bit suspicious and shy, with that dinner that occupied her hands – she was like an animal whose food might be taken from him; and the goiter seemed an animal in its own right, which, after having clawed at her trachea, was now drinking forth half her breath, hiding, however, under her skin like the photographer under his cloth. (*AG*, 52–3)]

Here Gadda creates his grotesque by deforming the normative sequence of naturalist (mimetic) description. His purpose is to undermine the self-sufficiency and homogeneity of his human object. The distortion is clearly meant to be offensive. By mixing the human, mechanical, and animal worlds, making them coexist and intertwine in the human fig-

ure, he objectifies what he (as author and the narrative voice of his mis-
anthropic protagonist) regards as the malevolent presence of the
masses. The grotesque is violent, comic satire: the goiter overwhelms
the individual, causing it to become puppet-like; like a hungry animal, it
attacks its prey, depriving it of its human spirit (the breath of which it
drinks), enveloping it and congealing its life into some non-human
aggregate, and finally, with the unexpected image of the photographer
hiding under his cloth, commenting obliquely on the photographic
exactness of the picture. These two sentences, so typical of Gadda's stylistic practice, have little enough in common with the Manzonian aesthetic of 'rettorica discreta' and 'buon gusto,' which, even in moments of
extreme ideological provocation, remains faithful to its rationalist
premises.[11] Nor does Gadda's grotesque attempt to mirror the kind of
natural, objective devastation of things we find in the Verga of *Mastro-
don Gesualdo*, where satire depends largely on the ruthless juxtaposition
of myth and material expediency. Instead, the purpose of the Gadda's
grotesque is to take the human subject to its extreme limits and in so
doing strike out against conventional narrative formulae (in the case
cited, both the benevolently comic [Manzonian] and tragic [Verghian]
stereotype of the peasant) – formulae founded on the belief, common
to modern character description, in individuality itself. There is no
doubt that Gadda's style is powerfully motivated by what he perceives
as violence perpetrated against his own self, and in *La cognizione* it is
plain that the narrator shares Gonzalo's contempt for all the beneficiar-
ies of his mother's love, thus the impulse to mock Battistina, who has
just received her daily ration of food from the Signora.

   In socio-aesthetic terms, the grotesque as practised by Gadda can also
be seen as a mirror for the degradation that art and the artist undergo
under industrial capitalism. The commodity status of culture is a natural barrier between the artist and reality, so much so that the author's
authentically mimetic impulses find no object on which to focus that has
not already been contaminated by its own cultural representation.
Hence distortion is not at all what it seems. Since the object is, on
account of its alienation from itself, an illusionary entity, a being whose
essence has been stolen, the author, not to fall victim to the illusion, uses
the degraded image against itself for the purpose of reinventing it. The
function of art, then, is to deliver the alienated object from its own
obsessions of unity and identity by focusing on its radical otherness. As
regards the autobiographical self which in Gadda is so resolute in its
desire to be known, its extraction from the rhythm of social life, its exist-

ence as a non-human recluse, and, at the same time, its rage are all means of grotesque representation. Put differently, once the habits and desires of heroic sentiment and romantic transcendence are checked, the authorial self can turn to and against the social order responsible for its non-being. Art thus allows Gadda to establish a different space between the supposed original and the deathly aspect of its material reality: namely, the space of satire.

Come la magia e la negromanzia conobbero il valore ossessivo o ricreativo della parola, così questa, anche nella società illuminata, serba il suo contenuto magico. Sta a noi di riscattarla dall'ossessione della frode e di ricreare la magia della verità. (*VM*, 453)

[Just as magic and witchcraft understood the obsessive and re-creative power of words, so, even in our enlightened society, words retain their magical content. It is up to us to free them from the compulsions of fraud and re-create the magic of truth.]

This is a revealing remark that has a strong bearing on Gadda's satiric art.[12] It states his belief that literary or poetic discourse, in particular, his own, is potentially (as it was believed to be in archaic or pre-logical societies) a powerful source of enchantment, capable of destroying false images in behalf of truth. As Frederic Jameson has argued in relation to Wyndham Lewis, a writer who shares more than one trait with Gadda, the modern satirist retains the fears associated with the magical curse of the image as he 'still obscurely believes in the annihilating force of his incantation.'[13] And like Lewis, Gadda shows a profound sense of guilt for the murders he (verbally) commits, which leads to a kind of sado-maschoistic attitude towards the representation of his autobiographical self. Misanthropy, in other words, elicits a self-caricature that borders on self-negation. It is clear, however, that the authorial self in Gadda is never truly negated. Gadda does not turn his aggressive impulses on himself completely, neither thematically in the sense that his direct auto-biographical projections become themselves victims of violent crime, nor stylistically with the brutality he reserves for other characters and things. Rather he subjects the self only to a kind of death-in-caricature, so that it retains its liminal status in order to safeguard the satiric impulse, which enables him to form, partially in *Quer pasticciaccio brutto de via Merulana* and wholly in *Eros e Priapo*, what Jameson calls an

'instinctual *combinatoire* or permutation system projecting all the logically possible variations on the basic structure of the aggressive assault implicit in satire'
(ibid: 142).

But Gaddian satire in its most developed form possesses a distinct feature that sets it apart from both ancient satire and the modern kind propounded and practiced by Lewis. While it carries out all the destructive and denunciatory functions of the genre in exposing the folly of human life, and while it does so, as Lewis preached, in a moral but not moralistic way, it does not constitute itself (as satire) according to any one point of view or any one particular style. What distinguishes Gadda from the satirists and macaronics of old, from Swift or Sterne, from Joyce, and from the variants of plurilingualism and humorous writing he could look to in his own native Italian tradition (Dossi, Faldella, etc.) is his practice of dispersing the narrative voice along a varied trajectory of different linguistic registers. By this I mean that Gadda's fiction texts are wholly decentred, deprived of an overriding consciousness that frames the narrative, which conveys the story's message either thematically or by means of the style it employs.

Criticism, beginning with Contini, has been keen on describing the 'fragmentary' and 'unfinished' quality of Gadda's work, particularly of *Quer pasticciaccio*, which, on account of its being conceived as a detective story, is all the more strange. On this matter, I agree with Stefano Agosti, who underscores the problematic nature of such a description. I shall return later to Agosti's reading of the *Pasticciaccio*, but first I would like to bring into this discussion some examples from Gadda's vast satiric holdings that centre on the human body. I have chosen this focus because the body is the main vehicle for the Gaddian grotesque and, more important, because, given the distinctly autobiographical character of Gadda's writing, the body can be seen as an allegory of the narrative and, in turn, of the authorial voice. The human body provides Gadda with an avenue to the root of existence, to life as object-reality, beyond meaning and discursive closure. In the cold objectification of life, the subject as an individuating force fades or disappears altogether.

Our first example is a short narrative entitled 'Anastomòsi,' in which Gadda describes a surgical operation, a resection of the duodenum. The scene is set in a university clinic. The narrator, admitted into the operating theatre as spectator (it is assumed that he is a medical student), is in a position to survey from above the work of a master surgeon. The narration unfolds as a commentary on the event, written in the margin of the patient's text: namely, his human body, anesthetized on the operating table. The whole narration takes place in a suspension ('un breve tumulto del mio sentire' [a short-lived commotion of feeling]). No referents are provided as to who the patient is, except a chart hanging from his bed indicating ('quasi incidentalmente' [almost incidentally]) his profession, which, however, is not disclosed. Hence, from the reader's standpoint, the patient is only a body subject to the surgeon's art and the narrator's probing gaze. The description is circular in that it mimics the circular process of the surgery. The patient is cut, opened up, his entrails displayed and then examined, the suspected diseased parts removed, then his body is sutured, restored to its original volume. The narration ends precisely with the final stitch which secures the contents of the body in their casing. What is striking in this piece is that its subject (anastomosis) informs the writing at every level: like the operation, the narrative voice severs and reconnects the subject's parts in an attempt to locate and identify a realty beyond closure, a kind of de-ideologized pure matter, mysterious and sacred in its unfathomable materiality. The surgeon's cut, much like the writer's, desecrates the mystery, the spirit (soul) of the person, to reveal the evidence of its physical composition, to understand nature's design. Like the painters of old who dissected human corpses to penetrate the secret of their form, the surgeon/writer makes his subject emerge through the disruption of its form – thus, the undermining of its metaphysics, its sacrifice which leads to its resuscitation:

Profanando il buio segreto e l'intrinseco della persona, ecco il risanatore ne ha evidenziato lo schema fisico: ha letto l'idea di natura nel mucchio delle viscide parvenze. Sul corpo disteso, disumanato, insiste con gli atti taciti della sua bianchezza: che mi appare quasi alta e muta madre o matrice della resurrezione. Ripenso, delle nostre antiche pitture, sant'Anna, sopra la Figlia, e Lei sopra il corpo illividito del figliolo.[14]

[Desecrating the secret darkness and the interior of the person, the healer has now outlined the physical schema; he has read nature's plan within the heap of viscid appearances. On the outstretched body, dehumanized, he insists with the silent acts of his whiteness, which seemed to me tall and silent mother or matrix of the resurrection. I think back to our ancient paintings, Saint Ann, leaning over her daughter, and She over the livid body of the son.]

In using the word 'subject' I am referring at once to the 'subject matter,' or focus, of the narration conveyed through the narrator's living consciousness of the event ('E l'ago avanza, avanza [...] Gli esseri del silenzio bianco, ora vedo [...] Carpiani, ecco, entra nella sala [...].etc. [And the needle advances, advances ... Now I see the beings of white silence ... Carpiani, now, enters the operating room]), not recollection, but simultaneity, and to the heuristic process embodied in the narrative voice. The question is one of how the subject represents itself and how it relates to the process of disruption and alienation it describes. The human figure lying on the operating table is, metaphorically, a text subject to transgression ('eviscerazione' [evisceration], 'spaventosa effrazione' [horrific infraction], 'nefando pasticcio' [wicked pastiche] are the terms used to describe the event). Before the body is cut, it suggests an unqualified, formal nakedness and the potential vulnerability of an unprotected surface. Therefore, it appears to have all the earmarks of a symbolic presence, governed by some moral law. The operation could be seen, mistakenly on my view, as an attempt by Gadda to depict dramatically the precariousness of the (ideal) human and, by extension, social body, rendered infirm by industrialization, democracy, and so on. In spite of Gadda's conservative politics and anti-democratic impulses, there are, as far as I know, no such instances of symbolic representation. Material or factual data do not enclose a meaning or truth that transcends them; hence Gadda's stated aversion to neo-realism and to other then-current varieties of realism, and his oft-stated fondness of what he regarded as the Manzonian 'grotesque.' Rather the body lying before the surgeon is (for the surgeon and his operating team) nothing but a body; it belongs to no symbolic or conceptual order; it is not regarded as a moral or ideological being and, since it does not speak, it is beyond language. The narrator, in fact, in a subtle disclosure of the author's viewpoint, states with regard to the surgeon's preparatory ritual: 'È strano: il gesto della indifferenza morale vien compiuto con la sollecitudine serena di chi ha preso conoscenza dei fini e dei mezzi, con la pacata insistenza della ragione' (*AN*, 331; Strange: that gesture of moral indifference is completed with the serene solicitude of someone who has the knowledge of ends and means, with the calm insistence of reason). Moral indifference, total knowledge of the process, guided by reason, which will lead to expulsion of the evil that prevents the body from functioning ('il modo proprio di chi ben sa e benignamente provede, ed escluderà il male dalla tenebra corporea e dopo gli esatti minuti vi ricomporrà le ragioni della vita' (ibid; the manner of someone who knows well and benignly provides, and will exclude the evil from that corporeal darkness and after the exact time has elapsed he will reconstitute the rationale of life). The cut body will then disclose its own order of reality, one that is 'undecidable' in terms of meaning, while at the same time being the source of enchantment: the repository of nature's secrets and mysteries, of an obscure, *material* profundity. We are at the beginning of the subject's eclipse as a signifying entity or discursive force and its remaking as an alienated object. But, as I shall illustrate, we are not dealing with the substitution of one element with another, with dichotomy and division, but rather with tension and contradiction.

Thematically, the body is a paradox. It emerges as the subject of the narrative at the very moment it begins its decline as the body of an individual, that is, as an epistemological and psychological centre of attraction; in other words, as a character. More important, its potential centredness is lost because the narrative voice has deprived it of a style consonant to its being. While Gadda maintains his point of view relatively fixed within the narrative frame of his voice as spectator and scribe, he destabilizes it through the deployment of different stylistic registers. Scientific and philosophical prose intersects with sublime and lyrical sequences, which in turn are interrupted by the comic and the grotesque. These multiple components of Gadda's language or stylistic codes are not employed with the purpose of creating a new unity of tone. Rather, in their movement between 'high' and 'low' styles, they highlight their incompatibility and strangeness with respect to any overriding stylistic norm. The sentence contains the alienation it is intent on describing:

I visceri venivano presi ed estratti come una sequenza informe di molli enigmi (per me), che i colori rosati, e rossi, e biancastri, e giallicci, mi dicevano appartenere all'attività prima e centrale della natura vivente. E questa non geometrica espressione dell'io vivo, già plasma, e negli anni organato da una 'idea' differenziatrice (tale sembrò nella immagine), l'operatore lo solleva d'una sua mano sopra le garze e la raggiera delle pinze, lo 'esteriorizza' nella chiarità dell'elettrico, frugandovi, frugandovi, come a volervi scoprire qualche ostinata reticenza, una simulazione pervicace, antica. Rigattiere dal bavaglio che cerca una moneta dimenticata in una vecchia veste frusta. Le dita ironiche sembravano palpare la frode. Ma non una goccia ne ricadeva, della calda porpora. Palese, a lui e ai suoi, nella celere veggenza degli atti in una lunga scuola ammaestrati, l'intimo e insostitutibile dispositivo della organicità; che si rivela invece così sconvolto, informe, superfluità rossa ed inane, o anzi miseria d'un pupazzo sbuzzato senza battesimo, alla mia cognitiva d'ignaro d'ogni antropologio e groviglio, smemorata di lontani studi, scarsa, incerta. (*AN*, 335)

[The viscera were captured and extracted; they seemed to me a formless sequence of soft enigmas; the pink, red, whitish, and yellowish colours told me that they belonged to the primary and central activity of living nature. And this non-geometrical expression of the living self, already made plasma, and over the years organized by a differentiating 'idea' (such the image seemed to me), the operator raises it with his hand above the gauzes and the radius of the forceps, he 'exteriorizes' it in the clarity of electricity, probing, probing, as if he were looking for some obstinate reticence, an ancient, stubborn simulation. A second-hand clothes dealer looking for some forgotten coin in an old thread-worn dress. His ironic fingers seemed to palpitate fraud. But he didn't lose a drop of the hot purple blood. Clear to him and to his team, in the rapid clarity of well- tempered movements, the intimate and irreplaceable mechanism of organicity; which instead reveals itself to my mind, ignorant of human anatomy and its complexity, and forgetful of bygone studies, insufficient, uncertain, dishevelled, formless, inane, red superfluity, or better the misery of a gutted, unbaptized puppet.]

The function of this stylistic practice is quite the opposite of what it seems. The narrative voice, intent on capturing the Real and reproducing it by combining its multiple elements, is, like the surgeon, faced with its ultimate inaccessibility. In coming face to face with the viscera of the human condition, the narrator can opt either to represent them in detail, knowing that in so doing he would fall victim to the illusion of their reality, their inauthenticity ('Le dita ironiche sembrano palpare la frode'), or to contaminate the object by deforming its appearances which are nothing other than the grotesque substitutes of phenomena, the external cover of some archaic essence, a plenitude beyond the realm of his discursive power. In the last analysis, the operation orders the patient's spiritual death, his depersonalization, into a kind of canvas for the author's satiric collage.

In this light, we see how Gadda brings the once dissipated subject back to centre stage and how its monadic isolation is ultimately defeated in comedy. The effect of such a repositioning, however, is that the subject disappears as a locus of meaning to become a locus of creation. As it gets lost in the text of satire, and as its parts are distilled in language, it loses its capacity to symbolize realities beyond its material form. This can be also viewed in those episodes in the novels where the narrator focuses on the human body as the scene of some inexplicable outrage. Where the body is made vulnerable to the narrator's gaze, it is not only objectified, but becomes something more than an object: the site of the creative play of language, the intersection of desire and reference, analogous to the operating table where the surgeon exhibits his creative energy in his search for some divine, magical essence. Among the many possible examples, two in particular are instructive: Gadda's description of the doctor's examination of Gonzalo that begins the third segment of *La cognizione*, and the dead body of Liliana Balducci in *Quer pasticciaccio brutto de via Merulana*.

The son is stretched out on his bed on a white blanket:

Su quel candore conventuale il lungo corpo e la eminenza del ventre diedero una figurazione di ingegnere-capo decentemente defunto, non fossero stati il colorito del volto, e anche lo sguardo e il respiro, a prevalere sulla immobilità greve della testa; che affondò un poco nel cuscino, bianco e rigonfio, tutto svoli. Subito la linda frescura di quello nobilitò la fronte, i capelli, il naso: si sarebbe pensato ad una maschera, da dover consegnare alle gipsoteche della posterità. Era invece la faccia dell'unico Pirobutirro maschio vivente che guardava alle travi del soffitto. Orizzontale sul bianco. Le due scarpe a punta, lucide, nerissime, parvero due peperoni neri, per quanto capovolti, puntiti. Movendo nelle àsole e nelle bretelle mani bianche, lunghe, il morto si preparava all'auscultazione. Dalla parete di fronte, tra le finestre, da una cornice di noce, la guardata corusca del generale Pastrufacio, in dagherrotipo. Vigeva a mezzo busto nella penombra, con il pon-cho, e due cocche alla spalla manca d'un fazzolettone sudamericano: e in capo quel suo berretto, tra familiare e dogale, cilindrico; torno torno esornato d'alcuni fregi di fil d'oro, in disegno di cirri, rare ghiande, viticchi. La bionda capellatura dell'eroe, schiaritasi molti anni avanti nel bagno di fissaggio, scendevagli armo-niosa alle spalle e quivi giunta si ripigliava dolcemente in una rotolatura nobilis-sima, da parer fatto d'Andrea Mantegna o Giovanbellino: come d'un paggio degli Este o dei Montefeltro venuto alle pampe, e agli anni di bandiera e di schi-oppo. Trascesa la cinquantina, tutte le gote e il disotto dei labbri s'infoltivano d'una generosità maschia del pelo, d'un vigore popolano ed antico: incrudito alla vastità delle guerre e superfluente dalle cornici dei ritratti.

La visita fu 'coscienziosa'. Il dottore palpò l'ingegnere a lungo, e anche a due mani, come a strizzarne fuori le budella: pareva una lavandaia inferocita sui panni, alla riva d'un goriello; poi, mollate le trippe, l'ascoltò un po'per tutto, sal-tellando in qua e in là, con il capo e cioè con l'orecchio, pungendo e vellicandolo con la barba. Poi gli mise lo stetoscopio sul cuore e sugli apici: per gli apici, sia davanti che dietro. Alternò l'auscultazione con la percussione digitale e digito-digitale, tanto i bronchi e i polmoni che, di nuovo, il ventre. Gli diceva: 'si volti': e di nuovo: 'si rivolti'. Nell'ascoltarlo dalla schiena quando era seduto sul letto e tutto inchinato in avanti, con il gonfio e le pieghe del ventre in mezzo ai femori, a crepapancia, e tra i ginocchi la faccia, la camicia arrovesciata al si sopra il capo come da un colpo di vento, oppure sdraiato bocconi, mezzo di sbieco, mutande e pantaloni senza piú nesso, allora il dottore aveva l'aria di comunicargli per telefono i suoi desiderata: gli fece dire parecchie volte trentatré, trentatré; ancora trentatré. All'enunciare il qual numero l'ingegnere si prestò di buona grazia, col viso tra i ginocchi. (CD, 620–1)

[On that monastic whiteness his long body and the eminence of his belly created an image of chief engineer decently deceased, except for the flush of his face, and also his gaze and breathing, which prevailed over the heavy immobility of his head, which sank a little into the pillow, white and swollen, all flounces. Its neat coolness immediately ennobled the forehead, his hair, his nose: one would have thought of a mask, to be turned over to the plaster-cast museums of posterity. It was instead the face of the only living male Pirobutirro who looked at the beams of the ceiling – horizontals against white.

His two tapering shoes, shiny, very black, looked like two black peppers, though upside down and pointed. Moving his long, white hands in the button-holes and the suspenders, the dead man prepared for auscultation. On the wall opposite, between the windows, from a walnut frame the coruscating gaze of General Pastrufazio, in a daguerreotype. He dominated, head and shoulders, the semidarkness, with his poncho and two tips of a South American kerchief on his left shoulder, and on his head that cap, somewhere between a homely head covering and a doge's hat, cylindrical; he was adorned all around with scrolls of gold thread in patterns of tendrils, rare acorns, filigree. The hero's blond hair, bleached many years before in the bath of fixative, flowed harmoniously to his shoulders and, once there, turned gently in a very noble roll, so that it seemed made by Andrea Mantegna or Giovanbellini: like a large page of the Estes or the Montefeltros come to the pampas, and to the years of the flags and muskets. He was well past fifty; both cheeks and the nether lip were thickened with a male generosity of hair; he showed a plebeian and ancient vigour – hardened in the vastness of his wars and overflowing from the frames of his portraits.

The examination was 'conscientious.' The doctor touched the engineer at length, and even with both hands, as if to squeeze the guts out of him: he seemed a washerwoman enraged with her laundry, at the bank of a little pond; then, having let go of the tripes, he listened to him everywhere for a bit, jumping here and there with his head – that is, with one ear – pricking him, tickling him with his beard. Then he put the stethoscope to his heart and his apexes, the apexes both before and behind. He alternated his auscultation with digital per-cussion and digito-digital, both the bronchia and the lungs as well as, again, the belly. He said, 'Turn over,' and then, 'Turn back again.' In listening to him from the back when he was sitting on the bed and all bent forward, with the swell and the folds of his belly between his femurs, to split his stomach, and his face between his knees, his shirt thrown over his head as if by a gust of wind, or else stretched out prone, half crooked, under drawers and trousers with no nexus then, at times the doctor seemed to be communicating his desiderata to him by telephone: he made him take deep breath after deep breath. And the engineer lent himself to this exercise with good grace, his face between his knees. (*AG*, 66–8)]

Here the crisis of the subject takes on one of many personal articula-tions found throughout the novel. As in the description of Battistina, we are dealing with the deformation of a naturalist aesthetic technique in such a way that the human object described, the son, becomes marginal to itself, as some kind of reified otherness. This focus allows the narra-tive to express the collapse of the individual subject on three distinct levels.

First, on the narrative level, in terms of point of view, it destabilizes the literary character by combining the reality of the individual with its surroundings so that, through caricatural insistence, it is transformed into something else. The body dissolves into the blanket and pillow, its face becomes a mask of itself, as the narrator constructs its degraded existence with comic reference to its shoes ('le due scarpe a punta, lucide, nerissime, parvero due peperoni neri, per quanto capovolti, puntiti') that at once stand out as signs of the protagonist's concern for his appearance amid the filth of his surroundings and as items of some phallic significance.[15] Such an association is meant to divert attention from the 'deep structure' of Gonzalo the patient, from his 'male invisi-bile,' his misanthropy, or his obsession with the memory of his dead brother. Its purpose is to show that the (thematically highlighted) iso-lated subject has lost its formal consistency because it has become the subject of a wandering, observing eye constantly distracted by objects that tempt its gaze. In fact, once Gonzalo is portrayed as corpse-like, the narrator's attention is drawn to another gaze, 'la guardata corusca del generale Pastrufacio, in dagherrotipo.' Thus between the reader and the spiritual categories of the protagonist is placed one more deviation, itself composed of numerous folds of historical and literary materials.[16] Then, in the actual medical examination, the subject is displaced at the literal level of the text as he becomes a virtual puppet whose degraded existence is caught somewhere between the laundry of the washer-woman and the ignominy of the doctor's scrupulous exploration; hence its caricature, a sign of its vulnerability, whether seated 'la camicia arrovesciata al di sopra il capo come da un colpo di vento' or stretched out 'mezzo di sbieco, mutande e pantaloni senza più nesso.' While the examination concludes that Gonzalo has nothing to worry about, it exhibits his degraded existence both as an object of knowledge and as the focal point of the narrator's gaze. The doctor's manipulation of the body becomes, in this respect, one with the author's semantic and for-mal manipulation, the effects of which lead to the text's structural 'inde-cidability.' The simple question of what is the narrator's point of view in regard to his subject cannot be easily answered.

The second level of dispersion is both psychological and psychoana-lytical. The narrative voice in *La cognizione* wavers between identifica-tion with Gonzalo, as here in the pathos conveyed in mentioning the 'letto più interno, il suo,' or in the closing comment on the examination scene, 'il malato si ricomponeva da un oltraggio non motivato nelle cose' and impersonal detachment, signalled by the medical inspection. Its description of the patient may be viewed as a way of defending against the power and intrusion of authorial emotion, an attempt to take possession of and control the self through satire. The authorial personal-ity, as refracted in the character of Gonzalo, exists in deep, self-imposed isolation; to protect that refuge and the psychological horrors it holds it must divert attention from itself (the real, but hidden, subject of narra-tion) by satiric depersonalization. The deadly force of writing, which ranges from playful to violent onslaught, is, in other words, an antidote to the 'male invisibile' (the hidden cause of the protagonist's malaise).[17] On the thematic level, the struggle between mother and son in the novel may be read in a particularly Freudian vein as a means of overcoming the Oedipus complex and thus as that point of entanglement at which the subject is produced and constituted and when it begins to accept reality, forsaking the pleasure principle and incest on behalf of culture. If there is anything that Gonzalo opposes it is the patriarchal law, and if there is anything he is deprived of it is the voice of conscience. Finally, Gonzalo has no specific gender role to play; he accepts no authority, nor has any desire to reproduce family and society, while, at the same time, he delays no satisfaction (his proverbial gluttony).[18]

The third level, which incorporates both the narrative and the psychological, is social. Gadda has repeatedly given his family's *déclassement* as the cause of his unhappiness.[19] On account of his father's imprudent investments, his family allegedly lost the bourgeois status it previously enjoyed. A recurring theme in Gadda's biography, this sense of having fallen down the social ladder is also crucial to the rendering of Gonzalo in *La cognizione*, particularly to an explanation of his contempt for the paternal villa. The anxiety generated by the loss of place is not, however, a class anxiety articulated in class terms (as is the case with Naturalism), 'the terror of falling into a social space that is radically Other' (Jameson 1979: 114), but rather an 'obscure sense that [his] own social space is contracting all around [him], that soon [he] will have no structural or institutional space of [his] own ...'(ibid). In this respect, what may be justifiably read as a symptom of the author's pathology projected on to his alter ego, Gonzalo, takes on a socially symbolic value. The crisis of the individual subject results from its being pushed out of the social space it had once commanded. Such a loss of place, the definitive loss of social status, is commensurate with the loss of the subject's textual space; its being made thing-like to be moved around by a narrator who, however, has no true voice of his own that would give some guarantee of representation. Other voices intrude to cloud the story's meaning. Hence, the loss/absence can be seen in the continual variation of point of view, in the lack of a wholly referential linguistic framework, and in the novel's ending that, while centring on the murder of the mother, gives the reader not the slightest clue as to who the killer might be. On the authorial level, the loss of social status, while no doubt explaining Gadda's anti-Socialism – which would be seen by him as the institutionalization of his loss – also explains his aversion towards the populist strains in the then ruling fascism.

Let us now consider our final example of Gaddian satire which takes the human body as its focus:

Il corpo della povera signora giaceva in una posizione infame, supino, con la gonna di lana grigia e una sottogonna bianca buttate all'indietro, fin quasi al petto: come se qualcuno avesse voluto scoprire il candore affascinante di quel dessous, o indargarne lo stato di nettezza. Aveva mutande bianche, di maglia a punto gentile, sottilissimo, che terminavano a metà coscia in una delicata orlatura. Tra l'orlatura e le calze, ch'erano in una lieve luce di seta, denudò se stessa la bianchezza estrema della carne, d'un pallore da clorosi: quelle due cosce un po'aperte, che i due elastici – in un tono di lilla – parevano distinguere in grado,

avevano perduto il loro tiepido senso, già si adeguavano al gelo: al gelo del sarcofago, e delle taciturne dimore. L'esatto officiare del punto a maglia, per lo
sguardo di quei frequentatori di domestiche, modellò inutilmente le stanche
proposte d'una voluttà il cui ardore, il cui fremito, pareva essersi appena esalato
dalla dolce mollezza del monte, da quella riga, il segno carnale del mistero...quella che Michelangelo (don Ciccio ne rivide la fatica, a San Lorenzo)
aveva creduto opportuno di dover omettere. Pignolerie! Lassa perde!

Le giarrettiere tese, ondulate appena agli orli, d'una ondulazione chiara a lat-
tuga: l'elastico di seta lilla, in quel tono che pareva dare un profumo, significava
a momenti la frale gentilezza e della donna e del ceto, l'eleganza spenta degli
indumenti, degli atti, il secreto modo della sommissione, tramutata ora nella
immobilità di un oggetto, o come d'uno sfigurato manichino. Tese, le calze, in
una eleganza bionda quasi una nuova pelle, dàtale (sopra il tepore creato) dalla
fiaba degli anni nuovi, delle magliatrici blasfeme: le calze incorticavano di quel
velo di lor luce il modellato delle gambe, dei meravigliosi ginocchi: delle gambe
un po'divaricate, come ad un invito orribile. Oh, gli occhi! Dove, chi guardavano? Il volto! ... Oh, era sgraffiata, poverina! Fin sotto un occhio, sur naso! ...
Oh, quel viso! Come era stanco, stanco, povera Liliana, quel capo, nel nimbo, che
l'avvolgeva, dei capelli, fili tuttavia operosi della carità. Affilato nel pallore, il
volto: sfinito, emaciato dalla suzione atroce della Morte.

Un profondo, un terribile taglio rosso le apriva la gola, ferocemente. Aveva
preso metà il collo, dal davanti verso destra, cioè verso sinistra per lei, destra per
loro che guardavano: sfrangiato ai due margini come da un reiterarsi dei colpi,
lama o punta: un orrore! Da nun potesse vede. Palesava come delle filacce rosse,
all'interno, tra quella spumiccia nera der sangue, già raggrumato, a momenti; un
pasticcio! Con delle bollicine rimaste a mezzo. Curiose forme, agli agenti: parevano buchi, al novizio, come dei maccheroncini color rosso, o rosa. 'La trachea,'
mormorò Ingravallo chinandosi, 'La carotide! La iugulare ... Dio!'

Er sangue aveva impiastrato tutto er collo, er davanti de la camicetta, una
manica: la mano: una spaventevole colatura d'un rosso nero, da Faiti o da Cengio (don Ciccio rammemorò subito, con un lontano pianto nell'anima, povera
mamma!). S'era accagliato sul pavimento, sulla camicetta tra i due seni: n'era
tinto anche l'orlo della gonna, il lembo rovescio de quela vesta di lana buttata su,
e l'altra spalla: pareva si dovesse raggrinzare da un momento all'altro: doveva
de certo risultarne un coagulato tutto appiccicoso come un sanguinaccio.

Il naso e la faccia, così abbandonata, e un po'rigirata da una parte, come de chi
nun ce la fa più a combatte, la faccia! rassegnata alla volontà della morte, appari-
vano offesi da sgraffiature, da unghiate: come ciavesse preso gusto, quer boia, a
volerla fregiare a quel modo. Assassino!

Gli occhi s'erano affisati orrendamente: a guardà che, poi? Guardaveno, guardaveno, in direzzione nun se capiva de che, verso la credenza granne, in cima in cima, o ar soffitto. Le mutandine nun ereno insanguinate: lasciaveno scoperti li du tratti de le cosce, come du anelli de pelle: fino a le calze, d'un biondo lucido. La solcatura del sesso...pareva d'esse a Ostia d'estate, o ar Forte de marmo de Viareggio, quanno so'sdriate su la rena a cocese, che te fanno vede tutto quello che vonno. Co quele maje tirate tirate d'oggiggiorno. (*QP*, 58–60)

[The body of the poor signora was lying in an obscene position, face up, her grey wool skirt and white underskirt flung back nearly to her breast, as if someone wanted to unveil the engrossing milkiness of that *dessous*, or investigate its state of cleanliness. She was wearing finely knit underpants, very sheer, that were bordered, mid-thigh, with the most delicate edging. Between the edging and her hose, impalpable and silky light, the extreme whiteness offered itself with the chlorotic pallor of denuded flesh; those slightly parted thighs to which the garters – in the shade of lilac – seemed to confer a distinction of rank no longer harboured any warmth; they were already disposed to the cold: the chill of the sarcophagus and of the voiceless abodes. The precise handiwork of the embroidery, to the gaze of those chasers of maidservants, emphasized uselessly the tired attraction of a voluptuousness whose ardor and whose shutter appeared to have just exhaled from the sweet softness of her mons, from that middle line, the carnal mark of mystery ... the trace that Michelangelo (don Ciccio mentally reviewed his labour at the Church of San Lorenzo) had thought it better to omit. Nitpicking! Fuhgeddaboudit!

Her garters were taut, though slightly frilled at the border in a candid lettuce curl. That elastic of mauve silk, in that hue from which a scent of perfume seemed to emanate, marked at moments the frail gentility of the woman and of her class, the spent elegance of her clothing, of her gestures, the secret mode of her succumbing, were now transformed into the immobility of an object, or a disfigured mannequin. Her stockings, taut in the blonde elegance of a nearly new skin bestowed (above the created warmth) by the modern wizardry of blasphemous knitting machines, her stockings girded with their sheen the shape of her legs and marvellous knees: her legs were slightly spread, as if in horrific invitation. Oh, her eyes! Where, and whom were they looking at? Her face! It was scratched, poor thing! Just under one eye, on her nose! ... Oh, that face of hers! Poor Liliana, how tired, tired, was her head in the cloud of hair that surrounded it, strands performing a final act of mercy. Her face was gaunt in its paleness, drained, emaciated by the atrocious suction of Death.

A deep, terrible red gash opened her throat, ferociously. It had taken half her neck, from the front to the right, that is towards the left for her, right for those looking on: its two edges gristly, as from the repeated blows of a razor or pick –

A horror! You couldn't stand to look at it. It brought to light what looked like red strands, inside, mixed with the black froth of blood, already clotted, nearly; a mess! With little bubbles congealed in the middle. Strange forms to the officers' eyes. To a novice they seemed like tubes, little red or pink maccheroni. 'The trachea,' murmured Ingravallo, bending over. 'Carotid! Jugular! ... My God!'

Blood was plastered all over her neck, on the front of her blouse, its sleeve: and one hand: a frightening wine-coloured stream from Faiti or Cengio (don Ciccio suddenly recalled with a distant cry in his soul: poor Mama!). It curdled on the floor, on her blouse between her breasts. There was also a stain on the hem of her skirt, on the underside of that woollen skirt flung back, and on the other shoulder. It seemed on the point of shrivelling up from one moment to the next. It was surely about to coagulate all gluey like blood pudding.

Her nose and her face, thus abandoned and slightly turned to one side, of someone who could no longer go on fighting, that face, resigned to the will of death, appeared scored with scrapes and fingernail scratches, as if that butcher got his kicks slashing her that way. Murderer!

Her eyes were fastened, atrociously: looking at what, then? They were looking, looking, in the direction of who knows what, towards the large buffet, the very top of it, or maybe the ceiling. There wasn't any blood on her panties. They left bare two bits of thigh, two rings of flesh, down to her stockings, glistening blond skin. The groove of her sex ... it was like being at Ostia in the summer, or at Forte dei Marmi or Viareggio, when the girls are lying on the sand baking themselves and they let you see whatever they want. With those tight bathing suits they wear nowadays. (*AM*, 67–70, with some variations)]

In a recent essay, Stefano Agosti cites this passage in support of his reading of Gadda, particularly *Quer pasticciaccio*, in the light of Lacan. Few readers would doubt that the question of the subject in Gadda, its place in society and its relationship to language, are suitable topics for Lacanian psychoanalysis. Agosti's argument, simply stated, is that the act of enunciating in Gadda does not disclose from what position or with what end in mind is something said. Just as we have seen above, the position from which Gadda's styles are generated cannot be clearly determined, and that 'undecidability,' according to Agosti ('la barra della mancanza di verità imposta da Gadda sulla forma dell'espessione, vale a dire sullo stile e, per ciò stesso, sull'ordine simbolico' [Agosti 1996: 258; the bar of the lack of truth imposed by Gadda on the form of expression, namely, on the style and, therefore, on the symbolic order]) gives Gadda entry into what Lacan calls the 'Real,' that is, that inaccessible realm beyond the reach of signification and therefore beyond representation and ideology: 'La descrizione del cadavere di Liliana Balducci costituisce il cuore di questa operazione, che si estende senza una falla, senza una fessura ("Le réel est sans fissure"... avverte Lacan), in una infallibile omogeneità, per tutto lo spazio del testo' (ibid: 258; The description of Liliana Balducci's corpse makes up the heart of this operation, which extends itself without a fault, without a fissure ['The real is without fissure,' Lacan remarks in an infallible homogeneity, throughout the entire text]). According to Agosti, Gadda's *Pasticciaccio* presents a simulacrum of the structure of the Real, that is, a structure devoid of both a foundation and an orientation whose internal logic is metonymically constituted. This would explain the dispersion of the narrative, the magnification of detail, and the deployment of elements that have no function whatsoever with regard to the novel's proposed focus. To buttress such a suggestive argument, Agosti cites Lacan's comment on the description of Irma's throat in Freud's dream: 'Il y a donc apparition angoissante d'une image qui résume ce que nous pouvons appeler la révélation du réel dans ce qu'il a de moins pénétrable, du réel sans aucune médiation possible, du réel dernier, de l'objet essentiel qui n'est plus un objet, mais ce quelque chose devant quoi tous les mots s'arrêtent et toutes le catégories échouent' (cited in Agosti 1996: 261; Thus we have the anguishing appearance of an image which embodies that which we can call the revelation of the real in that which it has that is least penetrable, of a real without any possible mediation, of the final real, of the essential object which is no longer an object, but something before which all words are mute and all categories fail). By analogy, Liliana's cut-open throat is a similar revelation of the Real, thus the suspension of meaning; the Real that for Lacan exists in strict conjunction with death. Liliana's throat so horribly disfigured is then, according to Agosti, the reverse image of her unfulfilled desire for maternity. One could also, as a parallel reading within the frame of Lacanian psychoanalysis, consider the description of Liliana's corpse as the figuration of a precious object (meaning) that is hunted for in vain. The narrative voice can never attain or possess it simply because it exists in the form of a metaphor, that is, as language. Its meaning can never   be truly established because it is regulated by the pulsations of the unconscious. The dead Liliana thus could be seen as a reflex of the human subject which is always dispersed in the discourses of which it is constituted.

The temptation to expose Liliana's corpse to psychoanalysis is indeed very strong.[20] However, a Lacanian reading of the description, while perceptive in accounting for Gadda's multiple stylistic registers, falls short of providing an adequate explanation of the specificity of the images contained in them. For sure, this description is engaged, like all other narratives according to Lacan, in the endless metonymic movement of desire, and Gadda's text, as Agosti argues, is a deliberate act of dispersion in which the Subject is irreparably dismantled. Keeping in mind this reading, let us now approach the description from the standpoint of its two most characteristic aspects: its abundance of sexual markers and its humour.

The position of the body on the floor demands that the narrator's cold, yet libidinous eye, return continually, as in a refrain, to Liliana's parted thighs, her underpants, the white flesh between her garters and stockings, the mons veneris and the mysterious line or furrow, 'la solcatura del sesso.'[21] The reader's attention is thus drawn to what for the philosopher-detective Ingravallo could be most disturbing: the sexual attractiveness of the murdered woman, her cold voluptuousness, an appeal which the narrative voice humorously deflects onto a register of detailed description, common to the purpose of any homicide report. The form the deflection actually takes, however, is in itself unstable. As soon as one descriptive norm or point of view is established, it gives way to another, leaving open once more the question of who is speaking or, better, what consciousness, or form of consciousness, the narrative voice is speaking through. It is reasonable to expect, given the work's conception as a 'giallo,' that the perspective is that of the detective, his investigative eye which, like the narrator in 'Anastomòsi,' surveys the scene in its every detail from above. The assumption in itself is sound because of the numerous points of contact and identification that exist between Gadda and Ingravallo. But if Gadda is the detective, he has transferred onto him the same cognitive dynamics, the same pulsations, the same play of unconscious drives and their relative forms of censorship, that characterize his writing in general. In other words, we could say that the enunciating subject (the narrator) attempts to imprint a specific law (a language) on an object that resists becoming the subject of the narrative and thus 'objectified' in one perspective. The constituted form becomes the object of verbal play from which the horrible outrage becomes comic spectacle. The formal play consists of various descriptive codes, from simple reportage of the kind to be found in a newspaper report ('Il corpo della povera signora giaceva ...') to a host of different points of view): polite curiosity ('il candore affascinante di quel *dessous*'), obsession with cleanliness ('lo stato di nettezza') and with refinement ('mutande ... di maglia a punto gentile'), mixed together with libidinous attraction ('le cosce un po' aperte'), scientific ('palore da clorosi') and poetic ('il gelo del sarcofago e delle taciturne dimore') reflection on death, and, of course, dialect. In Lacanian terms, one could say that Desire has dispersed the subject, made it swerve outward towards the desire of the Other into an impersonal frame or scene wherein the subject as a speaking consciousness is dissolved. But it is possible that the narrating subject has something else in mind. As it literally 'deconstructs' any pretense of centredness, as it displays its omissions and contradictions, as it produces divergent meanings, it does so with the manifest purpose of diverting the reader's attention from the object-ideal, Liliana, to its grotesque caricature, and thus of masking his obsession for the object by negating in humour its profound psychological appeal. The cancelling of one register for another can be seen as a form of negation, in the Freudian sense of *Verneinung*, that, while pointing to the repressed, signals the process of repression. The recurring movement from language to dialect (from norm to transgression), needless to say, is the principal source of humor in *Quer pasticciaccio*.

But within the brilliant polyphonic description of Liliana's corpse, there is an abrupt, and rather unexpected, swerve in the narration that brings the reader in contact with another stream of blood and another body: 'la mano: una spaventevole colatura d' un rosso nero, da Faiti o da Cengio (don Ciccio rammemoro' subito, con lontano pianto nell' anima, povera mamma!).' Here it would seem that Gadda has given to Ingravallo his own experience of loss, which may be summed up in William Weaver's gloss of the reference: 'Faiti and Cengio are mountains where the Italian army fought bitterly and suffered severe losses in the First World War, and where Gadda's brother was killed. For a moment, here, Gadda identifies himself openly with Ingravallo and attributes his own bereavement to the fictional character' (*AM*, 69). Hence in the many twists and turns that give the description its baroque figuration, we find one element that is constraining and reducible, and which constitutes what could be viewed as a trace of 'reference' and a possible clue as to why the narration was generated in the first place. Unlike a realist text, the description under consideration does not organize the relationship among its elements intelligibly, but rather foregrounds its own incoherences and transgressions as the natural and spontaneous movement of a narrating subject fragmented into several modes of consciousness. Thus the object of a critical reading of such a description is not to seek the multiplicity and diversity that the author is so willing to provide, but some unifying principle of generation that may account for the play of contradiction and that may be seen as a strategy to hide a potentially explosive 'content' behind the ruse of comic art. Several candidates from Gadda's biography amply qualify. At the top of the list are Gadda's deep identification with his mother and his fratricidal impulses towards his (dead) brother.

A useful way of approaching the description is to view it, in more traditionally Freudian way, as a form of free association. Placed before the image of a woman whose throat has been cut, the narrator says what comes to mind. What he utters is, of course, not uttered spontaneously (as in an analytical session), but is constructed as spontaneous. Let us suppose then that the viewing of Liliana's corpse sets into motion a series of personal associations which are too revealing not to be censored and for which there is no conventional literary code. Let us also suppose that Ingravallo functions as conduit and filter of these associations. In this sense, the detective is the source of the Other's perceptions and, as such, he can never really *see* what he *feels*. For example, it is not Don Ciccio who in fixing his eyes on Liliana's seductive deadness conjures in his mind the spectacle of Ostia or Forte dei Marmi in the summer,[22] but it is he who censors the intrusion of such a thought by deflecting it onto the consciousness of 'quei frequentatori di domestiche,' that is, the photographers and host of minor functionaries surrounding the body. However, in constructing his free association, the narrator must always remain to a certain degree outside of his construction. He does this by recoding the slaughter of Liliana as an outrageous act of cruelty in the form of another's discourse, so that the description appears as an ironic collage of different perceptions, and by intervening directly with ironic reference to literary sublimation, as when the gaze at 'il segno carnale del mistero' brings Michelangelo to Don Ciccio's mind, or when the scene of death activates the memory of Gadda's mother and dead brother. The latter intervention, however controlled it may be, is crucial because it involves another of the author's texts in which the detective is absent – namely, *La cognizione*, where mother and dead brother are principal reference points and which concludes with the murder of Gonzalo's mother. The trace of the other text is, as every student of Gadda knows, the trace of another trace and so on, as we move backwards in time from one work to the next. And although the trace may be seen to go beyond Gadda's writings (into, say, texts of writers such as Dostoevski and Céline, whose works Gadda knew well), there can be no doubt that the private sphere of the author's concrete experience is decisive here in the *Pasticciaccio* as elsewhere. But the point I want to stress is that Liliana's body, which we have viewed so far as an object deflected into different perceptions, may now be seen as the point at which meaning converges and is disseminated. In his interpretation of Leibniz, Deleuze makes the apparently cryptic statement that '[i]l n'y a pas de l'obscur en nous parce que nous avons un corps, mais nous devons avoir un corps parce qu'il y a de l'obscur en nous' (1988: 113; 'Nothing obscure lives in us because we have a body, but we must have a body because there is an obscure object in us' (1993: 85). 'The obscure object in us' is another way of decribing the subject of the *Pasticciaccio*. Liliana (in her absence) is that subject, a subject of its very nature dispersed because, as Deleuze goes on to say, in every monad there is 'une infinité de petits plis (inflexions) qui ne cessent de se faire et de se défaire en toutes directions'(115; 'an infinite of tiny folds (inflections) endlessly furling and unfurling in every direction'[86]). The fetishization and desecration of the body that produces here the grotesque is the means Gadda uses to transform his deepest anxieties and desires into a surface reality, a soulless piece of written matter devoid of affect, that is, into a negation-repression of the obscure. At the same time, the techniques that work the fetishization and desecration remain in full view as reminders of the obscurity the reader will never be able to decipher (e.g., Gadda's sexuality) for the simple fact that it comes without a local code, and that master codes, like those provided by Freud or Lacan, will in the final analysis not suffice. Liliana, therefore, allegorically speaking, 'is' nothing but literature: the more she is defiled by the gaze of the Other, the more suggestive (seductive) she becomes; the more she escapes the grasp of the dissipated subject, the more humorous her tragedy becomes; just as, while we are instructed by generic convention to look for a fictional killer, the text keeps telling us that the 'real' criminal is Gadda himself and that the scene of the crime is, like every other scene in the novel, the scene of satire. Sexuality and humour therefore take us to the heart of the masquerade; to a style that (like the criminal) escapes apprehension.

The samples of satire discussed above could be taken as proof of how Gadda abandons history and representation in favour of what has been called the 'pleasure of the text.' Although in many respects this may be true, it should not lead one to hold that there is no determinate meaning in Gadda's writings. 'Undecidability' is a strategy, rather than a cognitive principle by which Gadda abides. Gadda does not move from the premise that the identity of the subject is ruptured and diffused by the free play of language, but rather, inversely, that the relative free play of language is a highly suitable means of restoring an identity to a subject inhibited and terrorized by history. It is a surrogate identity, a mask to hide behind, but one that allows him to destroy the logic of narrative systems in which are embedded the social institutions deemed responsible for his malaise. This false self which does not lie, and which knows no identity except that of the Other, is the baroque subject of Gaddian narration.

4
A Baroque Ethics

Tu vuoi ch'io rinnovelli
Disperato dolor che 'l cor mi preme.

Dal poema del Belli il tempo e il costume vengono consacrati in una accezione di patimento, per un'acre o comunque drammatizzata immistione del personaggio nello incredibile fluire delle cose. E dal costume e dal tempo sgorga e incombe sul mondo, tra scoppi di irridenti risa e il serpere delle tentazioni e lo stagnare del peccato, dondola sul mondo la forma cupa del dolore. Vero ed assurdo come un incubo di Goya.

Emilio Manzotti has remarked that *La cognizione del dolore* charts an itinerary that consists of the subject's gradual acquisition in equal measure of *conoscenza* and *dolore*. The novel may be read, on his view, as a search for the ontological foundation of a single life, seen as the life of *everyman*.[1] In this respect, *La cognizione* has no doubt all the qualities of the modern epic, for which Joyce's *Ulysses* is the prototype. One is even tempted to recall Dante's journey in Hell, so eventful is the road travelled by the novel's protagonist and so grotesque are the representations we find along the way. Dante's journey, however, has a beginning and an end, and the world it describes is configured distinctly with mathematical precision. Grief is known through the experience of its many forms. Gadda's knowledge of grief is sustained by a different impulse. While Gadda's itinerary is no less moral than Dante's, it moves towards the possession of something obscure: a dark object, originating somewhere in the world, and contained by the knowing subject in the depths of its being, undecipherable. Unlike Dante, however, Gadda does not supply the referent of his loss by negating its presence ('la *diritta via* era smarrita'), but instead affirms the reality of loss by displacing that referent, disguising it in a myriad of forms which the more they are masked in satire, the more they draw attention to themselves. What appears, or can be reconstructed, as the autobiographical object has given itself over from the very start to a narrator who at once inhabits and estranges it, preserving it as a masked reality. In his hands, the autobiographical self turns into a means of accessing that very thing it endeavours to hide: its monadic existence as a fragment in a baroque world, a fragment which includes the world in order that it exist for the world.

La cognizione del dolore issues from a deeply seeded ethical paradox. Its subject is no longer a 'subject-in-the-world' responding to a universal moral imperative. Yet, at the same time, the subject attempts to stake out and defend an area of experience that depends for its very existence on what it does not possess – namely, individuality: an identity framed by a personal history within the sphere of the Other. Instead, the subject's life, which will be discussed as a metaphor in the person of Gonzalo, is limited to its inner being; what happens to it comes from the outside. In other words, the self and the world are two interdependent realms that do not interact: '[La] monade o io è la casa buia senza finestre [...] È il chiuso pensiero, puro, che non ha bisogno di luce dal di fuori, che ha in sé la luce [...]' (*MM*, 804; The monad or self is a dark house without windows ... It is thought sealed, pure, that has no need of light from the outside, that has light within itself ...) In itself, the monad is opposed to the world seen as a system of relations. It is indeed a dark room without windows or doors, but not, as Gadda would claim, impervious to light, for in effect different rays of light pass as through slits or cracks in a wall. These rays, instead of illuminating the room, create shadows that stand out in the very same way as dark colours stand out in baroque paintings to emphasize the obscurity. The obscurity belongs to the subject; it *becomes* the subject. At the same time, author and narrator know well that Gonzalo's monadic isolation is, cognitively (philosophically and logically), untenable: 'errore profondo della speculazione: di vedere ad ogni costo l'io e l'uno dove non esistono affatto, di veder limiti e barriere, dove vi sono legami e aggrovigliamenti' (647; It is a grave speculative error to see the 'I' and the one at any cost where they do not exist at all, to see borders and barriers where there are only connections and entanglements). And it is Gonzalo himself who unleashes against the pronoun 'I' the fiercest of all his tirades.

From an ethical standpoint then, monadic solitude is not an option, because, if in the dark room of his isolation Gonzalo does not look out onto the world, the world with all its relations and entanglements finds its way into his solitude. This situation produces a paradoxical inflection of the subject for which reality is at once obscure substance and entanglement. The paradox generates two equally distinct, but interrelated, expressive modes: the lyrical and the macheronic. The intersection and articulation of these forms of writing underlines the ethical dilemma at the heart of the novel: to negate or not to negate. The lyrical mode is the melancholic voice of the estranged, solitary monad, but who, through his narrating alter ego, exerts his power over the world of which he has been deprived by denying its meaning and denigrating its 'baroqueness.' The disinherited subject can see only the receding light of contingency ('la luce! ... che recede, recede ... opaca' [*CD*, 604; the light! ... which recedes, recedes ...opaque.)

The world that penetrates Gonzalo's dark cell of being is a world of lost objects. Affected by melancholia, the protagonist's mind wanders in pursuit of things he perceives as lost, that belong to the Other, and that, although real, have no meaning. These lost things are points on a vicious circle of life that attract and repel, and that often summon the reaction of the narrator, who exits from his position of omniscience, or assumed objectivity, to unite both with Gonzalo and his mother, causing a fusion of perspectives impossible to disentangle. There is no doubt that *La cognizione del dolore* is the story of the protagonist's love–hate relationship with his mother. But this conflict, however definitive it is as theme, does not give the novel its characteristic mark of style. However important the initial deprivation or loss might have been for Gonzalo (and the narrator), it does not explain his irrepressible hostility towards the outside world.

Our first impulse is, following the narrator, to configure the pain in relation to its object, Gonzalo, who suffers because he has been deprived. Carla Benedetti has taken this tack in applying the Freudian notion of mourning and melancholy to the text. Gonzalo's anger is an expression of the melancholy he feels for the loss of things assumed once to be possessed: 'Gadda's criticism of private property is a good demonstration of how this mournful recognition of reality works. Gonzalo, who never owned anything because everything was denied to him, manages to treat the wound inflicted on him by showing how illusory possessions are' (Benedetti 1997: 163). Accordingly, Gonzalo can also be viewed as a depressed narcissist who has been deprived not of this or that thing, but, as Julia Kristeva has written, of some 'unnameable,' 'supreme good ... something un-representable, that perhaps only devouring might represent, or an *invocation* might point out, but no word could signify' (Kristeva 1989: 13). In this respect, the excess of signification in the novel would be a direct result of a world perceived as bereft of meaning that must be devoured linguistically. Whatever means we use to decipher Gonzalo's malaise, there is no doubt that Gonzalo is the thing narrated, the 'supreme' object, lost to itself, but nonetheless ubiquitous. It is Gonzalo's being that pervades the text with all its perverse and masochistic movement. It is his gaze that penetrates into the uselessness of the world; his depression that governs the obscurity of the picture; his manic drive that negates the things lost by, paradoxically, reasserting their power over him: their capacity to bring forth linguistic omnipotence from the depths of his sadness. Yet the object-Gonzalo, in whom Gadda's life is rehearsed through its emblems of grief (brother, mother, father, villa), is overdetermined by a narrator who not only comments and judges his actions, but mocks and impersonates him as well, often identifying completely with him. The unpredictable conduct of the narrator contributes to the disquieting effect the novel has on the reader, an effect that becomes outright disorientation as we move through scenes that serve as pretexts for the bizarre and uncontrollable wanderings of the protagonist's mind. Hence what appears ostensibly as an autobiographical object is a fractured entity; its objectivity dismantled through a constant short-circuiting of its system.

The motive force behind what may appear as either delirium or fantasy ('delirio interpretativo' [interpretative delirium] or 'sogno gratuito alla don Quijote' [gratuitous dream a la Don Quixote]), Gadda insists, has a strong foundation in reality: 'nasce e discende [...] "dagli altri", procede dagli altri errori di giudizio e dalle altrui, singole o collettive, carenze di contegno sociale' (*CD*, 764; it is born and descends from others, from errors of judgement committed by others and from the collective or individual dearth of social conduct): Gonzalo reacts because he has been provoked; his linguistic action is fuelled by anger and resentment.[2] Hence his conduct stems from moral necessity. Gonzalo is therefore, in Gadda's interpretation, a modern-day Hamlet who punishes and, in punishing, vindicates the evil and outrage he has suffered, clearing the way to a possible future: 'Si noti che missione di Amleto, come quella di Oreste [...] è missione forzatamente negativa; punisce e cancella il male e l'obbrobrio, riaprendo al futuro la sua possibilità, la sua verginità' (*VM*, 153; Note that Hamlet's mission, like that of Oreste's, is forcefully negative: it punishes evil and disgrace, opening again the future to possibility, restoring it to its virginity). And, as in Gadda's reading of *Hamlet*, the 'ultimo Hidalgo' (an 'ultimo' that bears the weight of a moral imperative), Gonzalo is also engaged in a fierce struggle against the world as it is 'degli usi civili [...], della mensogna acquiescente, del patto ignominoso datore di salute fisica e di pace fisica' (of the civil customs ..., the acquiescent lie, the ignominious pact giver of physical health and peace) in behalf of a knowledge (the knowledge that causes the pain) 'dell'incarico e del conseguente adempimento cui siamo astretti dalle ragioni profonde del "cuore", cioè dall'imperio etico d'una ragione sopraindividuale: la coscienza etica dell'eternità' (152; of the mission and consequent fulfilment to which we are constrained by reasons deep within our heart, that is, by the ethical imperative that transcends the individual: the ethical consciousness of eternity). Gonzalo's aggression is motivated, Gadda tells us, not only by a world that has not responded to his pain, by a society and its guardians that have not given him the care he deserved, but also, and more important, by the 'imbecillagine generale del mondo [e] delle baggianate della ritualistica borghese' (CD, 764; the general idiocy of the world [and] the foolishness of bourgeois rituals) that have violated the closed, inner space of his melancholy. However, in contrast to Hamlet, who must choose between a life of adaptation to the lies of the world (non-being) and an ethical mission that could lead him to death – a choice that presupposes the mimetic integrity of the subject and does not, on my view, call into question the artifice of literature – Gonzalo's choice is between negating and not negating, that is, between deploying the artifice as weapon or not; not to do so would assume the validity of representing the object in itself, the world as it is. It would amount to accepting 'il bacio bugiardo della Parvenza, coricarsi con lei sullo strame, respirare il suo fiato, bevere giú dentro l'anima il suo rutto e il suo lezzo di meretrice' (CD, 703; 'the mendacious kiss of Appearances, to lie with her on the straw, to breathe her breath, to drink in, down into one's soul, her belch and strumpet's stench' [AQ, 171]). The world of appearances, like Dante's Siren, is a tempting object for the writer to pursue. But to seize on it would be equivalent to self-deception, a weakness of the will, and, what is more, a denial of the unconscious and the irrational side of human behaviour: 'Rivendicare la facoltà santa del giudizio, a certi momenti, è lacerare la possibilità: come si lacera un foglio inturpato leggendovi scrittura di bugie' (ibid; 'to vindicate the holy faculty of judgement, at certain moments, is to tear the fabric of possibility: as one tears an indecent paper, reading lies written on it' [ibid]). In the case of

Hamlet, the specific world of the referent is open to full view. What the reader chooses to do with the relationship of subject to the outside world is another matter. In Gonzalo's case, the Hamletic language of the narrator focuses not on the content of a specific thing negated, but rather on the process of negation itself.

As a reader of Freud, Gadda was most likely acquainted with his short paper on 'negation'– for no other reason than the passages cited above all refer to negation as a function of intellectual judgment. For Freud, negation was a way of becoming aware of what is repressed. Repudiation allows the ego sight of, but not acceptance, of the repressed: the intellect knows, but the emotions will not accept, and thus the repression persists. Hence the narrator, in charge as he is of Gonzalo's (and Gadda's) mind, understands that judging is an intellectual action that could lead to self-negation. Hence in a notably Freudian way, Gadda has juxtaposed two groups of instincts – Eros (affirmation/ acceptance) and Thanatos (destruction/negation) – to arrive, however, at a cognitive (and emotional) impasse: one cannot destroy the world of phenomena without destroying the self (which is also a vain image). To negate the self is to leave all hope behind (indeed, in the Dantean sense), thus putting an end to 'possibility.' Gadda uses the term 'possibilità' (like the terms 'Parvenza' and 'Negation') in the philosophical sense: that which is possibile is that which is not necessarily false (Aristotle). The narrator tells us that perhaps Gonzalo was about to 'negare se stesso' as a vendetta against the source, knowledge, and truth of his grief ('le ragioni del dolore, la conoscenza e la verità del dolore' [704]). In so doing, everything will have been said and done, consumed in the theft of grief ('Nulla rimaneva alla possibilità. Tutto andava esaurito dalla rapina del dolore' [ibid]). All that remains after the repudiative judgment are the signs of his contempt: 'Lo scherno solo dei disegni e delle parvenze era salvo, quasi maschera tragica sulla metope del teatro' (ibid). This last sentence has a double meaning and should be read not only as 'only the signs of falsity survive the process of negation' (Manzotti's edition, 356n), but also as: with the negation of self, only the signs of the subject's contempt remain – in the form of a tragic mask. In other words, Gadda's response (his parody and satire) to the world of phenomena is like a tragic mask hanging on a theatre's façade.

In *Totem and Taboo*, Freud asks a question about tragedy that would be fair to ask of Gadda's Gonzalo: why does the hero of tragedy have to suffer? Why does he bear the burden of pain, which, if he is meant to be a tragic hero like Hamlet, is one and the same with guilt? Of what then is Gonzalo guilty ? And why can he not find a remedy for his pain? The question is essential to any approach to the novel, for it places before us the emotional and psychical processes and dispositions of the narrative. It cannot go without notice that the narrator's Hamletic meditations on negation are couched in a web of images that include wet nurses, children playing in peaceful gardens, choir stalls, saints, farmers, unripe fruit, towers, and are followed by another bleak description of the hero's relationship to his mother. There is no nexus to these images, and they may be viewed as a kind of lyrical refrain of freely associated memories that collectively hark back to a different time ostensibly prior to the suffering, a time without guilt. The hero's love–hate relationship with his mother can, therefore, be summoned to provide an explanation of the simple Oedipal variety: the guilt, and thus the 'dolore' comes from his having committed the crime of wishing his father dead.

But such an interpretation does not suffice, for no other reason than it is what the narrator wishes the reader to believe. Gonzalo, we learn, despises his (deceased) father, referred to as Don Francisco in his tirades against the bells and the bell tower, and, as a show of his contempt, stamps on his portrait. But, most important, he displays repeatedly his hatred for the traces of paternal authority that, in one way or another, prevent him from having sole possession of his mother. The Oedipal triangle of Gonzalo, Mother, Father appears surely in place. Gianfranco Contini was the first to remark that the justification the narrator gives for Gonzalo's actions is utterly insufficient, if not useless. It is indeed true that the reader is made to suspect some violent, but undefined, childhood trauma that was caused by what he perceived to be a lack of motherly love. His resentment, Contini goes on to note, is fuelled by such petty and grotesque events as his father's financially unsound contributions to the construction of the town's bell tower, his mother's tolerance of parasitical domestics, and her giving of French lessons to her neighbours' lamebrained children, all of which, recounted through different narrative filters, produce a markedly comic effect. Contini is right to conclude that Gonzalo's neurosis is equipped with a typical self-defence mechanism which, like an allergic reaction, infects and at the same time protects the person afflicted. And it is this instinct of self-preservation that Contini sees as the cause of the novel's incompleteness. For Gadda to have completed his story would have 'contradicted the powerful solipsism that guarantees his literary vitality. A conscious descent into the Maternal Womb would have perhaps led Gonzalo to the supreme intellectual revelation characteristic of writers like Dante and Proust.'[3] Instead, Gadda, according to Contini, finds his salvation in humour which, ultimately, saves him from remorse and depression. What frees the text from the bounds of neurosis is the totally liberating laughter it generates.

The lack of cartharsis and the dissolution of a distinctively Freudian subject matter in humour are no doubt among the novel's most apparent features. Carla Benedetti, too, has underlined how unsatisfactory Gadda's hermeneutic of grief is compared with Proust's, and how Gonzalo's rage resists interpretation. To be sure, Gadda himself has not helped, referring to Gonzalo's malady as 'il male oscuro di cui le leggi e le universe discipline delle gran cattedre persistono a dover ignorare la causa, i modi: e lo si porta dentro di sé per tutto il fulgurato scoscendere d'una vita, piú greve ogni giorno, immedicato' (CD, 690; 'the obscure sickness of which histories and laws and the universal disciplines of the great chairs persist in having to ignore the causes, the stages: and one bears it within himself along all the resplendent descent of a lifetime, heavier every day, without medication' [AG, 154]). The degree of distance taken from the malady is, moreover, increased by parodic self-reference: the *Mirabilia Maragdagali* of a certain Father Lopez would appear to be nothing other than Gadda's own *Le meraviglie d' Italia*.

Yet in Gadda's work there are certain images and situations that recur perpetually and, thus, may help establish a perspective on the problem of the 'empty phenomenon' or absence of the object. Why does the autobiographical self experience anxiety before 'mere appearances,' when the fundamental empiricism governing its perceptions knows all too well that all we can know are appearances? Why the fear of materiality? Is the object best left dead? Gadda's compulsion to repeat certain situations in his prose derives from a need to restore an order of things that, as Freud would say, he is 'obliged to abandon under the pressure of external disturbing forces' (Freud 1989: 612). However true this may be in the case of persons in analysis, it is not exactly the case with literary creations, regardless of how autobiographical they are. The novel, in other words, is a way of managing the obscure fear, which is one and the same with the obscure evil (male), and at the same time indicating circuitously its cause. What is most important is that the obscure fear does not mark a direction towards death, an instinctual lunge back towards some transcendental totality (for Contini, the solution of a Dante or a Proust), but rather towards the self-preservation that can be achieved only through humour and satire.

Of the recurring ideas or motifs in Gadda's works, matricide is no doubt the most compelling. However, as Manuela Bertone has shown, matricide as an informing idea is more of an impulse than a structure; it exists 'in the margin of [Gadda's] texts ... in a space of partial darkness, in equivocation and ambiguity ...' (Bertone 1997: 111). The principal question Bertone asks is indeed crucial for any reading of *La cognizione del dolore*: why does Gadda, while suggesting the idea of matricide, withhold the crime proper? Bertone's essay argues, on my view very convincingly, that Gonzalo and his mother are involved in a destructive narcissistic bond which has dissolved 'the unity of the self into an undifferentiated state of identity and antagonism' (127). Gonzalo's impulse to kill his mother is therefore thwarted by the knowledge that her death at his hands would amount to the killing of self: 'the destruction of the biological and existential unit formed by two perfectly interconnected beings' (ibid). The repetition of matricide as a possibility, but not as reality, can thus be explained, from a Freudian perspective, within the dynamics of anxiety and repression. The matricide theme thus can be taken as a kind of allegory of the fear of castration. Gonzalo lives out the danger and the fear of his being disconnected from his mother by some external force (all the things of this earth in which the mother invests – chiefly, as we shall see, the memory of Gonzalo's brother who was killed in the war). This is a castration anxiety. The castration is, obviously, symbolic: Gonzalo, who has not emerged from the phallic phase of his attachment to his mother, feels threatened by the potential loss of his ability to unite with her. Gonzalo has repressed his fear of castration, while putting in its place his desire/fear for the loss of his mother. Macheronic satire and humour then serve as a double means of defence: they protect against accepting the external (social) world and its objects-emblems as meaningful in themselves; and they prevent, in their disruption of the lyrical mode, that the subject return to the comforts of its lost maternal attachment.

Yet, although the macheronic ultimately saves Gadda from the self-torture of melancholy, it highlights, by its very concern with presence (the brilliant surface of reality), that unfathomably lyrical dimension which in some way contains the subject's remorse and depression. Contini, in describing the phenomenology of Gadda's style, has pointed out that macheronic representation is usually preceded by a lyrical moment of nostalgia for something lost. The images produced are cast in extenuating rhythms and in words devoid of discursive meaning; syntagms are abstract, untranslatable, often interrupted by ellipses, and arrested at the height of their rhythm by exclamation marks.[4] The lyric mode then is both compulsive and fragmented; it is the vehicle of Gadda's anxiety, his sorrow, pain, and grief, the causes of which are silent, or at least buried in abstract allusion. Hence, we are forced to see the knowledge process in *La cognizione* as a vicious circle: it moves from absence (loss) to excess (presence) and back to absence: knowing is a grievous circle.

Federica Pedriali has attempted to find an exit in Gadda's cognitive labyrinth by identifying the cause from which the condition of perpetual conflict has developed. The principal subtext of Gadda's writings, the 'groviglio' he has chosen to disguise rather than unravel, is, she argues, his relationship with his dead brother, Enrico. Hence the eminently autobiographical *Cognizione del dolore* revolves around the dynamics of an Oedipal complex in which 'the third element in the triangle is Enrico, not Gadda's father' (Pedriali 1997: 137). Such a focus makes possible a different approach to Gonzalo's grief and, thus, to the meaning of the novel. Simply stated, Gonzalo suffers a pain that cannot be treated because it is too shameful to express: it is pain deeply rooted in the incontrovertible fact that his brother is the principal object of his mother's love, and that he can never aspire to becoming the centre of his mother's attention. Gonzalo exists in the shadow of life: 'condemned to darkness by his mother's perfidy [in choosing his brother over him], outshone by the blinding smile of his brother, no one acknowledges his moral superiority, neither Gonzalo's mother nor the rabble she protects' (150).

With Pedriali's insights and close readings, we are in a better position to map the crime with which the novel ends and understand why the criminal's identity can be suggested but never truly defined. Gadda's autobiographical projection, Gonzalo, hated his brother, who became the principal obstacle to his desire for total possession of his mother. After his brother had died and had become a symbolic presence in Gonzalo's life, he, as part of Gadda's autobiographical project, could not be represented, save as the absent cause of his malaise and thus of his mother's death: 'una cagione malvagia operante nella assurdità della notte' (*CD*, 754; 'a wicked cause operating in the absurdity of the night' [*AG*, 237]). Gonzalo, the reader is led to believe, was the instrumental cause of his mother's death, his dead brother, a hidden principle. In this way, Gadda preserves the ideal of his mother at the very same time, having assembled all the proofs of the outrages and miseries she has borne him, he is forced to destroy her; in addition, he saves the ideal of a brother who, on account of his mother's narcissism, he was made to see as the ideal son.

But what is more important for our discussion is a thematic constant that is a crucial determinant of the novel's form – namely, the refusal on Gadda's/Gonzalo's part to accept, or give way to, absence or loss. The lack Gonzalo feels is reflected not in a language that leaves empty traces of things that are nothing but words, as for example, in Pirandello, but in a compulsive, excessive filling of narrative space. Put differently, rather than capturing the nothingness of loss and reducing it to a formal principle of absence, Gadda imposes on that nothingness both plenitude and proliferation, an abundance of matter as a sign of his need to possess: a baroque excess which is not only a formal solution to nihilism, but an ethical one as well. Gadda is playing the Leibnizian game described by Deleuze:

c'est un jeu de remplissement, où l'on conjure le vide et ne rend plus rien à l'absence: c'est le Solitaire inversé, tel qu'on 'remplit un trou sur lequel on saute', au lieu de sauter dans une place et d'ôter la pièce sur la quelle on saute, jusqu'à ce que le vide soit complet. Enfin, c'est une Non-bataille, plus proche de la guérilla que de la guerre d'extermination, plus proche du Go que des échecs ou des dames: on ne s'empare pas de l'adversaire pour le rendre à l'absence, on en cerne la présence pour le neutraliser, le rendre incompossibile, lui imposer la divergence. C'est cela, le Baroque, avant que le monde ne perde ses principes: le splendide moment où l'on maintient Quelque chose plutôt que rien, et où l'on répond à la misère du monde par un excès de principes, une hybris des princi-pes, une hybris propre aux principes. (1988: 91–2)

[it is a game of filling holes, in which emptiness is imagined and where players refuse to give way to absence: it is an inverted solitaire, the player 'filling the square on which he lands' instead of jumping onto an empty spot, and remov-ing the checker he lands on until the board is empty. Finally, it is a non-battle closer to guerrilla warfare than a war of extermination, more like go than chess or checkers. You don't catch your adversary to reduce him to absence; you encir-cle his presence to neutralize him, to make him incompossible, to impose diver-gence upon him. The Baroque is just that, at a time before the world loses its principles. It is the moment when Some Thing is kept rather than nothing, and where response to the world's misery is made through an excess of principles, a hubris of principles, and a hubris inherent to principles. (1993: 68)

The 'hubris of principles' is the basis of entanglement, of proliferation, of an obsessive need to possess; there is no limit to abundance ('I doppi-oni li voglio, tutti, per mania di possesso e per cupidigia di ricchezze: e voglio anche i triploni, e i quadruploni, sebbene il Re Cattolico non li abbia ancora monetati: e tutti i sinonimi, usati nelle loro variegate accezioni e sfumature, d'uso corrente, o d'uso raro rarissimo' [*VM*, 95; The dubloons, I want all of them, on account of my mania for possession and cupidity for wealth: and I want the tri-bloons and the quadri-bloons, even though the Catholic King has yet to coin them: and all the synonyms in all their various meanings and nuances, in current or rare usage]). If Gonzalo's world has collapsed with the trauma of loss, Gadda will rebuild it, not as it was before, with its potential for ruin, but on a different foundation and according to different principles. In order that it correspond to the outrage, to the enormity of dispossession, it must be complete in all its complication and spontaneity. Hence once we have cited the causes of Gonzalo's grief and defined the process of grievous knowledge, its origins and effects, we think we have freed the text from its own obscurity, only to realize that we have been contaminated by the excess or infinity of that world which is not ours. Embedded in Gonzalo's consciousness, we are caught in the infinite series of the possible, but not absolute, abstract or pure, possibility – in this respect, Gadda is hardly the experimentalist he is claimed to be – but 'possibility' circumscribed by history, by a 'historical system,' Gadda's hidden God. The fabric of the text, Gadda's writes in 'Come lavoro,' depends only in part on cognition and impulse:

I fatti registrabili da una biografia esterna e, in modo più lato, da una storiografia dell' 'ambiente', sovvertono in misura orrenda, fino qualche volta ad annientarle, nobili costellazioni d'agganciamenti interni, dovuti all'operosità nativa dello spirito. Fatti fisici, urti e strappi, lacerazioni del sentire, violenze e pressioni da 'di fuori', ingiurie e sturbi dal caso, dagli 'altri', coartazioni del costume, inibizioni ragionevoli, estetiche ed etiche, dal mondo non nostro, eppure divenute nostre come per contagio, voi vedete, pesano siffattamente sull'animo, sull'intelletto, che l'uscire indenni dal sabba non ci è dato [...] La limpidità naturale dell'affermazione più nostra, più vera è devertita ed è imbrattata in sul nascere. Una mano ignota, come di ferro, si sovrappone alla nostra mano bambina, regge senza averne delega il calamo: lo conduce ad astinenti lettere e pagine, e quasi alle menzogne salvatrici. (*VM*, 429)

[Facts registered by an exterior biography and, in a more general sense, by a historical account of the 'milieu,' subvert horrendously – to the extent at times of annihilation – [those] internally connected noble constellations that emanate from the native operativeness of the spirit. Physical events, collisions and tears,

lacerations of feeling, violence and 'external'; pressures, injuries and disturbances, caused by chance, by 'others'; social constrictions, justifiable aesthetic
and ethical prohibitions of a world not our own, yet they become our own as
from contagion – you see, these all weigh so much on the spirit, on the intellect,
that to escape unscathed from the Sabbat is impossible. The natural purity of the
expression that is mostly ours, the truest and most amusing, is soiled at the very
moment it is born. An unknown, iron clad grip overcomes our childish hand,
holds without proxy the pen: it shows the way to words and pages of abstention
and almost to the salvational lies.]

In is in this sense that Gadda's texts are deeply autobiographical and
ethical, while at the same time governed by some supreme, iron-clad
force that dictates the absences and the 'salvational lies.' It is certainly
not by accident that the figure of Gonzalo is so elusive and that Gadda
has chosen to disguise him in the dress of several different literary figures from Oedipus to Don Quixote, Hamlet and Stephen Dedalus, as
Gian Carlo Roscioni has pointed out (1969: 168). By deflecting Gonzalo
into literature, Gadda has performed an important strategic move.
Romano Luperini has noted that at the most crucial moment in the
action, when the tension between mother and son is at its highest,
Gonzalo, incensed to find some local people in the house (they had
come there to bring his mother a basket of mushrooms), grabs his
mother violently by the arm and says '"... non voglio, non voglio maiali
in casa ..."' (CD, 736; 'I don't want ... I don't want pigs in the house ...'].
The senora, humbled, 'non osò alzare le palpebre. La parte superiore
della testa, la fronte, assai alta e le tempie, sopra le arcate degli occhi,
chiusi, parve il volto di chi si raccolga nella ricchezza silente e profonda
dell'essere, per non conoscere l'odio: di quelli che tanto ama!' (737; 'she
didn't dare raise her eyelids again. The upper part of her head, her
brow, high, and her temples, above the arcs of her eyes, closed, seemed
the face of one who is meditating in the silent and deep richness of one's
being, so as not to know the hatred: of those who are so loved' [AG,
214]). At which point, the narrator comments: 'Così riferisce Svetonio di
Cesare, che levasse la toga al capo, davanti la subita lucentezza delle
lame' (ibid; 'So Suetonius reports of Caesar, who raised his toga to his
head, before the sudden gleam of the blades' [ibid] ('utque animaadver-
tit undique se strictis pugionibus peti, toga caput obvolvit, simul sinistra
manu sinum ad ima crura deduxit, quo honestius caderet etiam inferi-
ore corporis parte velata': De vita Caesarum, I, 82, cited in Manzotti's edition, 436). The tragic tension of Gonzalo's final encounter with his

mother is displaced into the annals of literature. In the same vein, the tall, dark female figure that appears to Gonzalo in his dream reminds him of 'Veturia, forse, la madre immobile di Coriolano, velata'(CD, 633)(Veturia, perhaps the motionless mother of Coriolanus [AG, 83]), which causes the reader's attention to swerve for a moment to another text (Act V, scene 3, of Shakespeare's Coriolanus). To be sure, these literary references are not deployed as markers signalling the transcendent, imaginary world of literature; instead, the literary is exhibited ironically as artifice, as in the first example, or, as in the second, as some sublime locus of tragedy. In both cases, the literary provides Gonzalo's experience with a cover or mask, and, at the same time, it refutes any and all conceptions of literature as a consolatory refuge.[5] Gonzalo is so elusive simply because he has become a literary figure, aware of his own literariness. That is to say, the narrator constructs him as myth: misanthrope, enemy of the people, police suspect, wrathful, idle, gluttonous, greedy, and cruel. Stories, fuelled by the popular imagination, are recounted to illustrate his legendary reputation, mainly his cruelty and incurable gluttony. This is not to imply that there is some real Gonzalo who exists above and beyond what the people think. The deformed, comic image of the autobiographical subject given to the reader is not at odds with the author's. One is commensurate to the other, because one is the other. By making Gonzalo into a highly stylized literary character, and the novel into a pastiche of other texts, Gadda relinquishes any rational control he might have had over his character, or self-portrait. Instead, he inserts him into the world of objects and their complex and ambiguous relations. The character, like the text, is at once artifice and knowledge in progress (Luperini 1981: 491). The distancing achieved through objectification leads the reader to view the object in its myriad of relationships, contradictions, and affinities. As an object, or datum, it suffers the fate of all objects as a relational entity devoid of synthesis.

At the same time, Gonzalo's mythological stature is in itself parodic. Its greatness consists in the way it causes the reader to reflect on all the great character myths of Western literature, 'the prowess' and 'vitiating excess,' as Ian Watt has remarked, that have been crucial to our culture's development.[6] With Watt, we can think of Don Quixote's 'impetuous generosity' and 'limiting blindness,' Don Juan's 'boundless experience of women,' Faustus's 'curiosity' as opposed to Gonzalo's avarice and paranoiac suspicion, his willed celibacy, his doleful apprehension of the real; in a subtler vein, we can see how Gonzalo's 'inordinate egotism' has cast him, like Robinson Crusoe, away into isolation to become, in

sharp contrast to Defoe's hero, totally useless and certainly not a potential empire builder. When we think of how Gonzalo's character moves
against the grain of these character myths and how, in addition, it
exploits the post-Freudian reader's involvement in tragedy and neurotic
excess, we are in a better position to understand how Gonzalo embodies
a kind of absurd reinvention of myth that can take place only after every
illusion of subjectivity has been destroyed.

In this manner, Gadda moves between the opposite extremes of the
parody of myth and its revitalization through the estranged and distorted forms, symbolic of the degraded commodity culture of industrial
capitalism, junk materials left to be reassembled as clichés of a no longer
possible individuality. Take, for example, the extraordinary account
given of Gonzalo's gluttony through which Gadda executes on multiple
levels his parodic reinvention of character:

La quasi ferale aragosta raggiungeva le dimensioni di un neonato umano: ed
egli, con lo schiaccianoci, ed appoggiando forte, piú forte!, i due gomiti in sulla
tavola, ne aveva ferocemente stritolato le branche, color corallo com'erano, e
toltone fuora il meglio, con occhi stralucidi di concupiscenza, e poi di piú in piú
sempre piú strabici in dentro, inquantoché puntati sulla preda, a cui accostava,
papillando bramosamente dalle narici, la ventosa oscena di quella bocca! Viscere
immondo che aveva anticipatamente estroflesso a properare incontro l'agognata
voluttà. (*CD*, 601)

[The quasi sinister lobster assumed the proportions of a human infant: and he,
with a nutcracker, and pressing hard – harder! – both elbows on the table, had
fiercely crushed its claws, coral-colored as they were, and had removed from
them the best part, his eyes gleaming with concupiscence and then squinting
more and more inwardly, since aimed on the prey to which it neared, his nos-
trils flaring desirously, the obscene sucker of that mouth! – foul entrail which he
had in anticipation extruded to approach the longed-for voluptuousness. (*AG*,
42)]

Here Gadda rewrites what Freud called 'cannibalistic pre-genital sexual
organization,' and he does so in such a way as to involve the cannibal-
ism of Christian communion fiercely distorted in the gnawing of
Dante's Lucifer, as Niva Lorenzini has pointed out:[7] the act of devouring
'esito ultimo e iperbolico del mito della transustanziazione' (the final,
hyperbolic expression of the myth of transubstantiation). Gonzalo,
imprisoned in his infantile sexuality because deprived of his mother's

love, cannot separate sexual pleasure from the ingestion of food. While the sexual aim consists in the incorporation of the object, Gadda transforms his character's perversion into a bizarre spectacle through the hyperbole of myth. The hyperbolic narration of myth corresponds, needless to say, to Gonzalo's obsessive neurosis.[8]

For another, perhaps more useful, example of how Gadda distances the markedly Freudian content of his character's life, let us take a closer look at the theme of mourning and melancholia in *La cognizione*. Carla Benedetti, we have already said, has discussed this matter in detail, emphasizing the connections between the 'maccheronea' and melancholy: For Benedetti, the moments of comedy that enhance Gadda's work are a form of reconciliation with the things believed to be lost.'The laughter which punctuates Gadda's mournful recognition with its "precipitous transitions" is the same which may burst out during mourning and which psychoanalysis considers of a maniacal nature' (166). I will take a somewhat different approach. My first move is to reconstruct the Freudian narrative of melancholy in relation to the objectification of Gonzalo. As the Gaddian alter ego, Gonzalo, who feels the loss of his mother, takes refuge in 'narcissistic identification'; that is to say, he is left to reflect on his being alone in a world without meaning. At this point, as Freud maintains, 'hate comes into operation on [the] substitutive object (the narcissistic self), abusing it, debasing it, making it suffer and deriving sadistic pleasure from its suffering' (Freud 1989: 588). At the same time, the subject has regressed into identification with the lost object, on the one hand, while, on the other, he returns to the stage of sadism which expresses his ambivalent conflict. For Freud, sadism allows the melancholic subject an outlet from the quasi inevitability of suicide:

So immense is the ego's self-love [...] and so vast is the amount of narcissistic libido [...] that we cannot conceive how that ego can consent to its own destruction. We have long known, it is true, that no neurotic harbours thoughts of suicide which he has not turned back upon himself from the murderous impulses against others, but we have never been able to explain what interplay of forces can carry such a purpose through to execution. The analysis of melancholia now shows that the ego can kill itself only if [...] it is able to direct against itself the hostility which relates to an object and which represents the ego's original reaction to objects in the external world. (588)

Roughly configured, the self-love or 'I' against which Gonzalo so vehemently inveighs and which he projects onto the lost object (for Gonzalo, it is his mother's narcissism that has made him lonely and poor) is a condition of his own abandoned self, which has led him to the dilemma of self-negation. To preserve the subject, and to escape the certainty of its self-inflicted death, Gadda has to represent it as an object in the external world and to level against that object the metaphoric death provided by satire. The narcissistic libido is preserved paradoxically by means of its defamation. It becomes the expressive mode of the narrating subject, the 'interpretative delirium' or 'narcissistic rage' that destroys the Other through objectification, while protecting the self in the filter of self-caricature.

To illustrate let us examine perhaps the most notorious of Gonzalo's sadistic misdeeds: the account given of the torture he is alleged to have inflicted on a poor, unknowing cat:

Avendogli un dottore ebreo, nel legger matematiche a Pastrufazio, e col sussidio del calcolo, dimostrato come pervenga il gatto (di qualunque doccia cadendo) ad arrivar sanissimo al suolo in sulle quattro zampe, che è una meravigliosa applicazione ginnica del teorema dell'impulso, egli precipitò piú volte un bel gatto dal secondo piano della villa, fatto curioso di sperimentare il teorema. E la povera bestiola, atterrando, gli diè difatti la desiderata conferma, ogni volta, ogni volta! Come un pensiero che, traverso fortune, non intermetta dall'essere eterno; ma, in quanto gatto, poco dopo morì, con occhi velati d'una irrevocabile tristezza, immalinconito da quell'oltraggio. Poiché ogni oltraggio è morte. (*CD*, 598)

[Since a Jewish doctor, in reading mathematics in Pastrufazio, and with the help of calculus, had demonstrated to him how a cat (from whatever drainpipe it falls) can safely reach the ground on all four paws, which is a marvelous gymnastic application of the theorem of impulse, he at various times hurled a lovely cat from the third floor of his villa, a curious way of testing the theorem. And the poor little creature, upon landing, in fact gave him each time the desired confirmation, each time! Like a thought that, through every vicissitude, never ceases being eternal; but in so much as it was a cat, it died shortly thereafter, its eyes veiled with irrevocable melancholy, saddened as it was by that outrage. Because every outrage is death. (*AG*,38)]

Gadda's narrative practice, in the passage just quoted, involves a complex process which Pier Paolo Pasolini has analysed from the standpoint of style. Gadda constructs an initial pastiche of Ciceronian Latin ('avendogli [...] dimostrato'), Renaissance syntax ('nel leggere matematiche,' 'di qualunque doccia cadendo'), and the combination of high and low usage (the etymologically rare 'doccia' and the more urbane 'che è una meravigliosa applicazione ginnica del teorema dell'impulso'), only to transform the pastiche into an allegorical narrative which contradicts the premises on which the original narrative is based. Pasolini maintains that Gadda resorts to the pastiche as a means of defending himself against '[un]mondo che si presenta orribilmente oggettivo, nemico, precostituito nella sua lingua strumentale, o istituzionale o anche letteraria' ([a] world that appears horribly objective, an enemy, pre-constituted in its practical, institutional and even literary language: Pasolini 1963: 63). Gadda, in other words, takes refuge not in the principal imitated text (as would, say, a Renaissance humanist in his imitation of classical Latin), but in the comic deployment of a third language (Renaissance latinate syntax). Although true, the defence appears to be more of a diversionary tactic than a means of escape. Gadda certainly wants to give the impression that someone else is writing, but that someone else who is writing is writing about him.

There are two languages at work in this passage, as in the rest of the novel: a language of the already known, which the reader can identify as alien and, thus, suspect (the pastiche), and the private language of *dolore*. The pastiche frames the writer's desperate experience in such a way as to render it visible but not comprehensible. Hence the reader is purposefully estranged from the text not because he cannot guess the meaning of the allegory, altogether manifest in the concluding 'Poiché ogni oltraggio è morte' – namely, as Pasolini remarks, that it is not the cat that has suffered the tortures of the sadistic Gonzalo but Gadda himself ('in realtà non è il gattino, ma il Gaddino, o il Gaddone, che viene defenestrato' [66]); the reader remains disoriented because he realizes that the story is recounted in a code foreign to him and, consequently, that there is no basis for communication between him and the text, no starting point in a process which helps him reproduce Gadda's inner vision. The solitary, self-reflecting subject has constructed his narcissistic defence, reinforcing his isolation and fragmentation, while at the same time isolating the reader, cutting him off from meaning.[9] This is essentially Gadda's revenge against the outrages suffered, against his repeated deaths: 'over and over again' as in Gonzalo's legendary torturing of the desperate cat. In this way, the subject, having become the object of its own narration, directs against itself its deeply seeded hostility.

The metaphoric death of the subject, however, is – it is worth repeating – the essential precondition for the reinvention of narrative. Pasolini had chosen to write on the passage because it represented for him an exceptional example of linguistic reserve, devoid of the expressive fireworks one usually associates with Gadda's writing. His reading collates the various aggregates of Gadda's pastiche in order to demonstrate its stylistic complexity. But why the pastiche in the first place? It functions no doubt as a means of psychological disguise, but while it does that very thing, it also puts into practice a totally new conception of narrative. Much has been said and written on Gadda's indebtedness to tradition, to classical literature, Machiavellian-style prose, to Folengo and Rabelais, to romantic elegy, to naturalism and symbolism; for Gadda these are all languages, thus raw materials, building blocks, that one can move around at will for they are all part of the world of language just like, as he writes in 'Belle lettere e contributi delle tecniche,' '[i] piú oscuri processi della conoscenza individuale e collettiva' (the most obscure processes of individual and collective knowledge). or '[gli] ultimi fatterelli della nomenclatura e della terminologia, [le] definizioncelle d'un dizionario tecnico e d'un quadro murale per classi d'artigianato' (the ultimate petty items of nomenclature and terminology, the brief definitions of a technical dictionary and of a wall section for teaching laborers: *VM*, 78). The pastiche of Renaissance Italian prose is a means of reviving old modes of cognition not – as Fredric Jameson writes in his considerations on Wyndham Lewis's pastiche of Elizabethan language –'in some first degree representational narrative, but rather within that second degree of speech which is the theatrical language of the characters of the now dramatized original paradigm and which it thus stands, less as its mimesis, than as its implicit and explicit commentary' (1979: 68). In Gadda, the 'theatrical language' of estrangement belongs to the narrating subject who transforms the potentially realistic narrative into a sign system that at once reveals and absorbs the cruelty of the protagonist's sadistic impulses, impulses which reflect back on the writing process itself and on the technique (the pastiche) which ensure the 'perpetual freshness' (Jameson 1979: 75) of that process.

It is at this point that we must attempt to address the reasons behind the pastiche. What motivates Gadda to thrive on deception by giving the reader the false impression that someone other than he is writing? A stylistic practice that depends largely on citation and on the intricate combination and entanglement of linguistic codes can in no way be regarded as 'spontaneous' or 'sincere,' let alone 'realistic.' The passage we have commented on in terms of its style contains the answer to this question in the very event it describes – namely, the *fall*. Federica Pedriale has persuasively shown that the legendary act of cruelty recounted here is meant to evoke the death of Gonzalo's brother.[10] But no matter how strong the biographical implications of this passage might be, they are not sufficient in explaining the allegorical meaning of the cat's perpetual plunges. The *fall* to which Gadda is referring, the *outrageous* fall to *death*, is the fall of the subject into reification, into a thing-like existence devoid of meaning, thus into its monadic isolation. The stylistic practice exhibited in the passage, and throughout Gadda's works, is a form of aesthetic production aimed at overcoming the privation. Hence what presents itself as loss from a psychological standpoint – the referents are numerous: maternal love, financial dignity, class affiliation, country, career, and so on – combines with the loss of language itself, which derives from the writer's inability to reproduce the object-world of his experience.[11] Things, objects, and events, the raw materials of narrative discourse, for Gadda appear as vital elements in a degraded world. Imprisoned in a world of commodity exchange, they are themselves devoid of meaning. Their value for narration consists in their potential for being something else: 'Cose, oggetti, eventi, non mi valgono per sé, chiusi nell'involucro di una loro pelle individua, sfericamente contornati nei loro apparenti confini [...]: mi valgono in una aspettazione, in una attesa di ciò che seguirà, o in un richiamo di quanto li ha preceduti e determinati' ('Un'opinione sul neorealismo,' in *VM*, 629; Things, objects, events have no value for me in themselves, enveloped in their individual skin, spherically framed by their apparent borders [...]: they have value for me as expectation, as a waiting for something to follow, or as a recall of something preceding or determining them.)

So at the centre of Gadda's stylistic practice we must position the themes of loss and sadism, and their attendant motifs. Gadda's expressionism derives from his awareness that the real is inaccessible, but at the same time still can be reproduced as illusion (as opposed to 'Parvenza') marked by its own illusiveness. Hence Appearance – to return to Gonzalo's dilemma of negating or not negating – is taken and deformed by putting in its place its own caricature. The pastiche then may be viewed as a means to enhance the caricature, in fact to define it as such.

There is, however, one thing in external reality that the narrator must face as real and factual, and that cannot be transformed into, or disguised as, something else – namely, death. It is not an accident that *La cognizione* stops with the image of death, but not death itself. Gonzalo's mother is mortally wounded, attacked in her bed by, it is assumed, an intruder. She shows so few signs of life that one wonders why Gadda did not choose to end the novel with her actual death. One can subject this final choice to different psychoanalytical interpretations, but in so doing I think the true importance of the novel's ending will be missed. The following passage evinces the heart of *La cognizione*:

Ora tumefatto, ferito. Inturpito da una cagione malvagia operante nella assurdità della notte; e complice la fiducia o la bontà stessa della signora. Questa catena di cause riconduceva il sistema dolce e alto della vita all'orrore dei sistemi subordinati, natura, sangue, materia: solitudine di visceri e di volti senza pensiero. Abbandono. (*CD*, 754)

[Now swollen, wounded. Debased by a wicked cause operating in the absurdity of the night; with the Senora's trust and her very goodness as accomplices. This chain of causes led the sweet and lofty system of life back to the horror of the subordinate systems, nature, blood, matter: solitude of viscera and of countenances without thought. Abandonment. (*AG*, 237)]

Beneath this debased and deformed surface, in the silence and barren solitude of matter, there is a principle of recuperation. The character has become the object and the event, has undergone the metamorphosis that death promises. Tumescent and mortally wounded is not only Gonzalo's mother, but a whole process of life, the supreme value, a formidable existence that succumbed to social routine and convention in such a way as to contribute to its own extinction, now fallen prey, as it has, to more fundamental systems. The senora is not dead, because, in her having been overcome by some cruel fate, her accident signals her entry into the complex workings of a material cosmos, into the web of causes and subcauses, into the infinite dimensions of the universe, into the chain of events, actions, thought, determinations; in sum, into an infinitude of creative possibilities. In this system into which the senora has passed, there is no place for the ideal or for myth; the structure of events rules out completely any and all representations of character. This passage sets before us Gadda's mature aesthetic. What he describes lying on its death bed is the entire tradition of narrative art and language which he has caused to swell into caricature, denigrated and deformed, made the object of the whirl of his schizophrenic vision. Let this reality now rest in peace; but how, one is justified in asking, how can any dignity be regained when identity has been erased? 'Parve a tutti di leggere la parola terribile della morte e la sovrana coscienza della impossibilità di dire: Io' (CD, 755; 'It seemed to all that they could read the terrible word of death and the supreme awareness of the impossibility of saying: I' [AG, 237].) Therein lies the pain: how does the monad live, when its solitude has been abandoned? Its experience is now the dead letter of art.

5

A Baroque Mystery

In contrast to *La cognizione del dolore, Quer pasticciaccio brutto de via Merulana* has at its centre not the individual, autobiographical subject whose force can be measured by its neurotic intelligence and by the strength of its obsessions, but rather a city: Rome, capital of Italy and seat of the Fascist government and law.[1] At the same time, the form and conventions of detective fiction adopted (and parodied) by Gadda provide a means for both the amplification and the objectification of the nameless referent at the basis of *La cognizione*. In this sense, *Quer pasticciaccio* extends and formalizes the thematic nucleus of *La cognizione,* while distancing the investigation onto a territory in effect more alien to the author's spirit and upbringing (because geographically real) than the South American setting, depicted parodically in the image and likeness of Gadda's native Lombardy.

Italo Calvino has written that the *Pasticciaccio,* more than a murder mystery, is a philosophical novel, based on a conception of the world as a 'system of systems':

The seething cauldron of life, the infinite stratification of reality, the inextricable tangle of knowledge are what Gadda wants to depict. When this concept of universal complication, reflected in the slightest object or event, has reached its ultimate paroxysm, it seems as if the novel is destined to remain unfinished, as if it could continue infinitely, creating new vortices within each episode. Gadda's point is the superabundance, the congestion, of these pages, through which a single complex object – the city of Rome – assumes a variegated form, becomes organism and symbol. (Introduction to *AM,* vi)

The 'universal complication' Calvino notes derives from Gadda's philosophical intelligence: his ability to see relations and correspondences among things and to execute what, in one of the most important treatises on baroque poetics, Gracián calls the 'artificiosa conexión de los objetos'[2] (artful connection of objects). The objects of Gadda's world are not only material objects, but also, and primarily, objects of thought or modes of signification. By choosing to set his novel in the multilingual city of Rome, Gadda draws his raw materials from an objectively real context in which Italian is combined with Roman, Neapolitan, Molisan, and a host of other dialects and sub-languages that make up the linguistic theatre of Roman life. The 'artificiosa conexión de los objetos' consists of the dialectic established between local speech and the narrative voice. The narrative system that results from a combination of incongruity, dissonance, and juxtaposition can be seen no doubt as dialogical, as in the sense attributed to the term by Bakhtin. Gadda distorts the primary event of the crime into the banality of everyday life and speech; but the bizarre entanglements that result from his unpredictable linguistic transformations release the power of the individual subject to graft onto the grotesque surface it has created, and over which it rules, its own private language of grief.

Gadda's choice of writing his novel as a *giallo* can be explained, on the one hand, by his predilection for detective fiction,[3] and, on the other, by the more immediate circumstance of a crime actually committed, the Stern murder, the newspaper accounts of which may have stimulated his imagination.[4] These factors, however important in establishing the origins of the novel, tell us little about how Gadda manages the epistemological functions of the genre. First, since detective fiction embodies the social process of policing people and institutions, surveillance is its immediate objective. The authorial voice of *Quer pasticciaccio* appropriates this function, which, in the traditional detective novel, belongs to the police. Ingravallo, Dott. Fumi, Maresciallo Di Pietrantonio, and the agents nicknamed Lo Sgranfia and Er Biondone, in addition to Brigadiere Pestalozzi of Marino, carry out the policing in its own right, while, at the same time, they are part of the object-world under close surveillance by the authorial voice. The purpose of this latter investigation is not simply the drawing of attention to commonplace and banal things that could be related to the crime. Rather, the probing inspection of everything and anything is Gadda's way of expanding the network of causality *ad infinitum*. In other words, Gadda's intention is not to construct, *à la* the nineteenth-century novel, a minute system of causes, but, through perpetual displacement, to create a parody of the need for causal exactitude and specification that we can see displayed so typically in the positivist-inspired detective fiction of a Conan Doyle or the French

feuilletonistes. In this respect, Gadda's originality consists less in representing the tangled scheme of things which in traditional detective fiction begs to be, and is usually, unravelled, than in expanding
entanglement in such a way that solution and closure are virtually
impossible. In this regard, even the simple inquiries made to confirm
information provided by a suspect, as in the case of Liliana's cousin
Valdarena, who was the first to find her body, branch out into unfore-
seeable designations. To illustrate, the reasons Valdarena gives for his
being on the scene of the crime are validated by the Roman office of
Standard Oil, where he is employed: he was indeed about to be transferred to Genoa and had stopped by Liliana's house to say goodbye. A
brief (ironic) account of Valdarena's qualities is given and restated by
the narrative voice: 'Un elemento piuttosto sveglio, buon parlatore
quando voleva, dal far distinto' [...] (94; A rather alert type, good talker
when he wanted to be, distinguished in his manners). It would be
expected, according to convention, that the inquiry either would put the
detective's mind to rest, or would have provided some clue to
Valdarena's possible involvement in the crime, which is not the case.
Instead, the concluding pages of Chapter 3 chart the movement of
Ingravallo's mind on the subject of Valdarena and have little or nothing
to do with the specific crime of Liliana's murder. As everywhere else in
the novel, the narrative progresses by means of solicitations. The
thought of Valdarena's business success, his good looks, and his seductive ways with the ladies prompts the satiric replay in the detective's
mind of what was, presumably, said to him at the office of Standard Oil
in defence of their product and their employee. So the inquiry unexpect-
edly folds out onto how prospective business clients are like women
who have to be seduced ('Bisogna che s'innamorino della Standard: che
imparino ad aver cieca fiducia nella Standard Oil' [They have to fall in
love with Standard: they have to learn to place blind faith in Standard
Oil]) and from there onto a long satiric account of the specifications for
the types of oil produced. Here is an excerpt from the passage much too
long to quote in its entirety:

'Il nostro gran segreto, vede, è quello che ci piace di raccontare a tutti: *la costanza
dei requisiti per ogni determinato tipo di olio.* Prenda, per fare un esempio, il nostro
imbattibile Transformer Oil B marca undici Extra. Può chiederne, all'ingegnere
Casalis dell'Anglo-Romana: all'ingegner Bocciarelli della Terni.' Si aiutò coi diti
della sinistra, pollice, indice, medio, scartandoli uno dopo l'altro ad elencare i
meriti della marca undici: arrivò al mignolo dove rimase: 'Anidricità assoluta: è

un requisito essenziale: va bene: condizione sine qua non: temperatura di conge-
lamento ... bassissima: viscosità ... 2,4 Wayne, a far tanto: grado di acidità, tras-
curabile: potere dielettrico, stupefacente: punto di infiammabilità ... il più
elevato di tutti gli oli industriali americani.' (QP, 96)

['Our best-kept secret, you see, is the one we tell everybody: *The firmness of our
requisites for every determined type of oil.* Take, for instance, our unbeatable Transformer B Eleven Extra Oil. You can get double confirmation of that from engineer Casalis of the Anglo-Romana Division, or engineer Bocciarelli at Terni.' The
fingers of his left hand came to his aid, thumb, index finger, middle, ticking off
one after the other the merits of Eleven Extra until he stopped at the pinky,
'absolutely anhydrous, the essential criteria. Fine. The *sine qua* non, rock bottom
freezing point; viscosity, 2,4 Wayne, at most; degree of acidity, negligible; dielec-
tric strength, amazing; flashpoint, the highest of all American industrial oils.']5

The policing force has been transferred from the detective to the
novel's master voice, which blends so perfectly with the former's frame
of mind that it cannot be distinguished from it. By this time in the novel,
the reader can sense the jealousy Don Ciccio feels towards the hand-
some and well-to-do Giuliano. And anyone familiar with Gadda's other
works will have no difficulty connecting Don Ciccio's feelings to
Gadda's satiric treatment of similar types who revel in the fast pace of
the modern, industrialized world: dynamic, unmelancholic, seducers of
life in general, and of women in particular. But now the policing has
passed from the banality of Valdarena, his temporal presence in the
economy of the investigation, to the even more banal pretensions of the
capitalist enterprise of Standard Oil, to the spacial extension of the narcissistic desire of possession. However, while Gadda, the detective, surveys with his infallible super-vision Valdarena's business habitat, his
purpose is much less to produce a full knowledge of the character than
to produce a spectacle of useless knowledge. This is just one section of
the large area of irrelevance which detective stories uncover in order to
restrict meaning in the assignment of guilt. With Gadda, however, this
universally suspect area is where the true guilt lies. Valdarena is the
conduit between the specific crime and the mass psychology which justifies the crimes of the Fascist state.

'Innamorare il cliente! Ecco tutto. Per fargli entrare in testa la verità! Nient'altro
che quello. Il dottor Valdarena, quanto a chiodi, ha manifestato buone disposiz-
ioni. Il giorno, poi, che si sono innamorati, e che hanno provato il Trasformer B,

è ben difficile, creda, che si lascino sedurre: che si lascino tentare a metterci le corna! E poi, corna a parte, chi ci ama ci segue: e allora ... Una sigaretta?' 'Grazie.' 'Allora, magari, voglio dire, pagano. Pagano senza rifiatare.'

'Pagheno, pagheno,' grugnì don Ciccio, nella solitudine del proprio foro interiore. (97–8)

['Win the client's heart! That's all it takes. Hammer the truth into his head, the long spike of the truth. And our Valdarena's good with a hammer. Once they're in love, and they've tried Transformer B, they're not about to lose their heads over somebody else and go cheating on us. And then, cheating aside, who loves us follows us. So then ... Cigarette?' 'Thanks.' 'So in that case, then, they pay up. They pay up without so much as a squeak.'

'Pay up, pay up,' grumbled Don Ciccio, in the solitude of his inner forum.]

Second, the genre operates on the basis of posited norms which crime subverts. These are the essential presuppositions of all detective stories, and especially of those written prior to the *Pasticciaccio*. The ideal world, represented as absent or impaired in detective fiction, needs to be policed so that it can retain its ideal status. When the police appear on the scene of the crime, it is a sign either that the fabric of normality has been torn and needs to be repaired or that it is tenuous and requires protection. In any case, the presence of police in the novel is a sign that the community is vulnerable.

Gadda locates his story on via Merulana in the grey, everyday world of the Roman bourgeoisie. The fact that the law in the person of Don Ciccio first visits this locale as a friend of the Balduccis solidifies the domain as co-natural to its (and his) presence. In the traditional detective story, when such a space is violated, it does not give itself over to delinquency, but instead enforces its own system of class habits and security. In *Quer pasticciaccio*, the investigation respects no limits whatsoever. The middle-class community in which the crimes take place would normally feel safe after it is initially disrupted by the police investigation; the crime, in other words, is a dramatic exception to the rule, as is the presence of the police. By locating the criminal and assigning culpability, the community can return to normal life: once the tear in the social fabric has been mended, a certain resiliency is felt gained. Life can resume in innocence. There is no innocence in Gadda's novel, no person or object that does not fall subject to the creative renaming of the authorial gaze; no *zona franca* immunized against parodic reinvention.

Before any crime is committed, the reader from the very first pages knows that nothing is safe, and soon will realize that the knife that cut so merciless into Liliana's candid flesh is but a metaphor for the writing process itself.

Hence what we experience in *Quer pasticciaccio* is a cognitive procedure diametrically opposite to the common epistemology of the traditional detective story. Although the narrator, like the police, is engaged in monitoring the world he has created, its close surveillance is not aimed at enforcing the rule of law or the norms on which society rests. So in Gadda's text there is no clear distinction made between what is normal and what is deviant. Rather, the investigation moves from the premise of a society in ruin, where in some way everything has deviated, or is separated, from some moral or societal norm. The deviance is in fact the norm. Love, for example, is represented by homosexuality, necrophilia, masturbation, and, possibly, incest, practices that are never depicted, but rather alluded to in a mostly comic vein. It would, in fact, not be exaggerated to say that Gadda is obsessed especially with sexual deviancy, while, nevertheless, being careful to assign to his characters, rather than to the narrative voice, most sexual references and innuendos – to Don Lorenzo Corpi, for instance, from whom we learn about the indecent habits of Liliana's young maids. It is only when the politically deviant, in the form of Mussolini and fascism, is evoked that Gadda's own voice is heard. But here also, in the many diatribes against Il Duce, sexual allusions are deflected in satire. In any case, it is the form of Gadda's *giallo*, not his interest in sexual deviancy, that concerns us here.

As D.A. Miller has shown, the classical detective story is based on the premise that *'everything might count*: every character might be the culprit, and every action or speech might be belying its apparent banality or literalism by making surreptitious reference to an incriminating Truth' (1988: 33). However, in the last analysis, 'the criterion of total relevance [...] invoked by the text [...] turns out to have a highly restricted applicability in the end' (ibid). A close reading of Gadda's final chapter will illustrate the nature of his conclusive solution and, therefore, of his police story. In formal terms, the question amounts to whether things actually come together and reveal the existence, however tenuous, of a plot structure, or whether, as most critics hold, we are left with the fragments of a hypothetical solution.

First of all, it is useful to keep in mind that the *Pasticciaccio* is a story about two crimes and, therefore, of two investigations, which give rise to two mutually entangled plots and two solutions.[6] The story is articulated on a purely temporal basis, by days and, as we near the conclusion, by hours: the theft of Signora Menegazzi's jewels takes place on Monday, 14 March, Liliana's murder, three days later, on Thursday, 17 March. The first seven chapters describe the crimes, preliminary inquiries, and the interrogation of possible suspects. Chapters 8 to 10 are devoted to the quest inspired by the clues and investigative rationale. Pestalozzi, Santarella, and 'er Biondone' all move into action, the jewels are recovered, the culprits identified, and, with the exception of Enea Retalli, apprehended. Chapter 10 is composed of three sections, each of which relates the activities of the police in pursuit of Liliana's killer, presumably Retalli. In the first section, after a relatively brief paragraph describing the course taken by Santarella towards Pavona and Palazzo, the localities in the direction of which he believed Retalli had headed, the investigation moves back to Rome, where Er Biondone is ordered to Piazza Vittorio Emanuele, Rome's market square, in search of Ascanio Lanciani, a possible accessory to the crime, whom he apprehends at the stand where he and his grandmother are at work selling *porchetta*. In the second section, we are still in Rome, but now with Don Ciccio, whom we follow on the morning of 23 March as he wakes up and attends to his toilette and breakfast, devoutly prepared by his landlady, and then to pick up the car in which he and four agents drive to Marino. The last part of the chapter takes place outside of Rome, mostly *en route* from Marino to Tor di Gheppio, the village-abode of Assunta Crocchiapani, the maidservant of the Balduccis who was in service the evening Ingravallo had been invited to supper, over a month before, on occasion of Remo's birthday. Don Ciccio believes that Assunta knows who the killer is and hopes to force her to divulge his name. The chapter ends with a visit to a room in which Assunta's father is lying on his deathbed. Assunta does not reveal the killer's name, and the investigation (with the novel) ends, presumably, in paralysis.

In his recent book on the *Pasticciaccio*, Ferdinando Amigoni has given the novel, particularly its final chapter, an interesting Freudian reading. Briefly, his argument is as follows. Detective Ingravallo assumes that the killer is male and the maidservant's lover (Enea Retalli). Assunta, he supposes, told him about Liliana's wealth. But when Don Ciccio tries to get her to say his name, she, in a moment of high emotional tension, cries out 'No, sor dotto', no, no, nun so' stata io!' (No, Doctor Sir, no, no, it wasn't I!) Amigoni, with Freud''s concept of *Verneinung* in hand, concludes that indeed it was she, not her boyfriend, who slit Liliana's throat. In her cry, the voice of the repressed Other is supposedly heard. Assunta does not reply to Don Ciccio's question, but rather to another question generated in her unconscious mind through a kind of 'metonymic short-circuiting' (127), which she resists by negation. She therefore confesses her guilt by denying what she has repressed. This is all quite plausible, especially for a writer like Gadda, no doubt familiar with Freud's essay on 'negation,' and so committed, as he is himself, to travesty and deception. At the same time, we must be cautious in turning the Freudian key too quickly. The situation is only virtually one between analyst and analysand, lest we consider all police interrogations of this kind, and not every cry of denial is necessarily a sign of guilt. Why does Assunta then respond to a question that she was not asked? First of all, Don Ciccio does not ask her whether she knows the murderer's name; rather, assuming that she does, he tries to force her verbally to confirm something the police already know: '"Fuori il nome!" urlò Don Ciccio. "La polizzia lo conosce già chesto nome. Se lo dite subbito," la voce divenne grave, suasiva: "è tanto di guadagnato anche pe vvoi"' ('"Out with his name!" yelled Don Ciccio. "The police know this name already. If you tell it right now," his voice became deep, persuasive: "it's all to the good, for you"' [387]). She replies that she knows nothing; Ingravallo insists that she does and threatens to take her in; at that point, she cries out that it was not she. A simple reading of Assunta's response is that she is, as Ingravallo thinks, lying: she knows the killer's name, but in uttering it she would implicate herself as accomplice. Thus her cry could mean Yes, I was involved, but did not actually kill her, or it could mean simply that she is innocent. In any case, whether she is the killer or accomplice, or whether she is innocent, cannot be determined at this point in the narrative. Don Ciccio appears to be struck by her resiliency and vitality, paralysed, and perhaps repentant of his aggression, of the outrage of interrogation. This reflexive hiatus in the narrative is not a conclusion, and one would expect that the narration, and investigation, would resume. The black, vertical fold 'tra i due sopraccigli dell'ira, nel volto bianchissimo della ragazza' could hint to a fold in the tissue of the narration, as it signals a sudden shift in the frame of reference, a dramatic transition unto another register. We are at the verge of knowing the name of the killer, but it has not been given yet. We are on the threshold of resolution, waiting for the ultimate phase.

Unlike traditional detective stories, *Quer Pasticciaccio* (at least in what we have of it) refuses to name the obscurity it relates. It makes no difference what Freudian readers suspect, the *Pasticciaccio* does not simplify its working complexity to provide a solution. But if it is true that we are about to unravel the mystery and, thus, move into the realm of order, it is equally true that Gadda at this very point blocks movement, doing so after the investigation or detection process has exposed not only the social and institutional orders in which the crimes take place, but the human and material orders as well. What drives the narrative off on to the innumerable tangents it comprises is a pervasive desire to disclose the secrets hidden behind the façade of things. But what motivates Gadda's baroque spectacle and propels the complex machine of detection can only remain the object of hypothesis and conjecture. By refusing to assign guilt, Gadda compels the reader to remain within the sphere of the desire behind the narrative action, a desire gratified in the investigation and that centres on the transgressive sexual activity that takes place at the heart of the mystery within the Balducci family between the lovely Liliana and her many adopted nieces. Narrative desire then becomes itself doubly transgressive, because, while it exposes the transgression, it subverts the formal codes (of the detective story) that prevent transgression from becoming the norm, bypassing the need for closure and the restoration of order. It is now that one is inclined to make the methodologically problematic jump backwards into the personal sphere of the author: to his repressed homosexuality and to his transvestitism; to his alleged love–hate rapport with his mother; to the jealousy he felt for his brother killed in the war; to the guilt–remorse dynamics generated by such relations; or to Gadda's oral obsessions manifested in his renowned gluttony. But once this is done, one has put a stop to the whole reconstitution process: to the unfurling of possibility according to which reality is captured but not imprisoned in closure.

Perhaps the best way to understand the *Pasticciaccio* is, following Deleuze, to understand in what way the baroque is a 'transition': 'Le Baroque est l'ultime tentative de reconstituer une raison classique, en répartissant les divergences en autant de mondes possibles, et en faisant des incompossibilités autant de frontières entre les mondes. Les désaccords qui surgissent dans un même monde peuvant être violents, *ils se résolvent en accords*, parce que les seules dissonances irréductibles sont entre mondes differénts' (111; 'The Baroque represents the ultimate attempt to reconstitute a classical reason by dividing divergences into as many worlds as possible, and by making from incompossibilities as many possible borders between worlds. Discords that spring up in the same world can be violent. *They are resolved in accords* because the only irreducible dissonances are between different worlds'[81–2]).The question then is one of accords without closures; between the active perceptions of a roaming narrative mind and the story line, set by convention. Let the descriptive sequences in the final chapter suffice to illustrate how divergences are resolved by a textual machinery that produces a story from the natural movement of its constituent parts while at the same time transformimg the story into projections that emanate from the authorial viewpoint. The universe of the novel has lost its centre, but not its unity, as, for example, il Biondino and his field of work. The description comprises numerous clusters or aggregates that lend to the action a formidable excess, but the distribution or collection of phenomena are not the result of random observation; rather, they are linked to one substantial component of the story (il Biondino), the young dapper agent who enjoys playing the role of the idle sleuth. At the same time, these descriptive aggregates have an inner unity which governs their movement, a movement which is virtually infinite. Here is one segment of this movement loaded with derivative forces that project out into private phenomenological categories of authorial experience: in this particular case, the usual objects of Gaddian satire (housewives, good-looking young boys) combine with a gourmand's eye for food:

L'indomani alle dieci esatte il Biondone era in loco (dopo aver dato una giratina fra i palmizi): è l'ora che le donne sogliono provvedere a mercato, in vista non solo della cena, quanto anzitutto del pranzo alle cure loro imminente: l'ora delle mozzarelle, dei formaggi, delle vermìfugge cipolle, e dei cardi, sotto la neve pazientemente ibernanti, degli odori, delle insalatine prima, dell'abbacchio. Gente che venneveno la porchetta su le bancarelle de piazza, quela mattina, ce n'era na tribbù. Da San Giuseppe in poi è la staggione sua, se po dì. Col timo e co li fiocchetti de rosmarino, e l'agli nun ne parlamo, e il contorno o il ripieno de patate co l'erbetta pesta. Ma il Biondo, a capo ciondoloni, si lasciò condurre tra i berci e le arance rosse dal suo dinoccolato ottimismo, sufolando in sordina, o atteggiandovi appena appena le labbra, tacendo a un tratto, levando un occhio in qua e in là, come a caso. Oppure sostava chiotto chiotto, la lobbia giù a metà fronte, le mani in tasca, la gobba infreddolita sotto pastrano chiaro fresconcello, aperto, e dietro i due polsi cadente, da parer coda di marsina. Era un pastranuccio di mezza stagione fasulla, che tirava al peloso, e al morbido, e riusciva liso in più punti: contribuiva a definire l'immagine d'un bellimbusto assonnato, in cerca di una cicca da poté fumà. Involtato nel turbine degli inviti e degli incitamenti alla compera e in tutte le conclamazioni di quella festa formaggia, trascorse piano piano davanti le bancarelle abbacchiare, oltrepassò carote e castagne e attigue montagnole di bianco-azzurini finocchi, baffosetti, nunzi rotondissimi d'Ariete: ivi insomma tutta la repubblica erbaria, dove alla gara dei costi e delle profferte i novelli sedani già tenevano il campo: e l'odore delle bruciate in sul chiudere pareva, dai pochi fornelli superstiti, l'ordore stesso dell'inverno fuggitivo. [...] (253)

[The following morning, precisely at ten, Blondie was on the spot (after having taken a little stroll among the palms): it is the hour when housewives are used to doing their marketing, with a view not only to supper, but more especially to the midday dinner, which is their imminent care: the hour of mozzarellas, cheeses, vermifuge onions, and cardoons, patiently hibernating beneath the snow, spices, choice salad greens, goat meat. There was a tribe of people selling roast pork from stands in the square that morning. You might say that from the feast of San Giuseppe on it is its season. With thyme and bouquets of rosemary, not to mention garlic, accompanied or stuffed with potatoes and diced herbs. But Blondie, with his head hanging, allowed himself to be led among the cries and the red oranges by his loose-limbed optimism, whistling softly, or putting his lips in position to do so, suddenly silent, casting an eye here and there, as if by chance. Or else he stood still, inconspicuous, his Homburg halfway down his forehead, hands in his pockets, his chilled back under a light-coloured and rather lightweight coat, open, and with its two sides drooping in the back till it looked like the tail of a full-dress coat. It was a phony between-seasons topcoat, which inclined towards the hairy, and to the soft, and proved worn in many places; it helped create the image of a drowsy wastrel, looking for a butt to smoke. Wrapped in the vortex of invitations and incitements to buy and in all the conclamations of that cheese festival, he moved slowly in front of the goat stands, passed carrots and chestnuts and adjacent mounds of bluish-white fennel, slightly moustached, rotund heralds of Aries: there present, in short, the whole republic of herbs, where in the contest of prices and offers the new celery already led the field: and the smell of the burny chestnuts, at the end, seemed, from the few remaining braziers, the very odour of winter in flight ...]

Here, in this conventional moment of unravelling, as throughout the text, the story exceeds its frame; the detection process becomes compressed, interiorized in the personal moods and humours of the authorial voice. Hence the investigation is extended beyond all reasonable limits and marks a space where the world's contents are unwrapped and exhibited. The result is that the text combines the individual beings represented as the forces in the investigation (here Il Biondino, later Ingravallo and fellow agents) with other forces which appear as monadic clusters of possibility: the depths of matter, drawn into clarity, link the reader to the obscurity of the investigation. As the elements of a material universe find unity in their collective extension, they spill over their specific frames to engulf the story in such a way that it is given a new consonance which affirms but does not resolve. Put in terms of the detective story, the authorial voice itself interrupts the police functions by creating other domains beyond the laws of the genre which cause the powers of detection to deflect away from the centre into a variety of pockets of representation, all marginal and beyond surveillance. The investigation then, instead of mending the tissue of deviance by solving the crime, underlines the authorial crime which crystalizes in the aberrant scenes of description. As a result – and this is the principal ideological effect of *Quer pasticciaccio brutto de via Merulana* – the concept of delinquency is radically altered. If it is true, as Miller argues, that the traditional detective story, by 'confining the actions of the police to a delinquent milieu ... reinforces the ideology of delinquency' (1988: 4): that is to say, it strengthens the social norms by punishing the guilty who dare invade the realm of order and middle-class tranquillity, then, in Gadda's novel, by contrast, delinquency occupies the same space as the police, but, since it is one and the same with the process of detection, thus capable of multiplying *ad infinitum*, it itself becomes the norm. In this sense, the continual mocking of Mussolini and the laws and pretensions of the Fascist state may be considered as one of the many delinquent objects in the text, a cluster of folds that multiply at will, filling the emptiness of a collapsed world. In other words, delinquency, all that is left of a society in crisis, constitutes the other (baroque) stage of representation.

It is by now a commonplace in Gadda criticism to regard the Gaddian text as wholly meta-linguistic: poly-semantic, polyphonic, interdiscursive, intertextual; that language for Gadda is not a means of representing reality, but rather an attack on linguistic convention in behalf of the heterogeneity of the sign and the multiplicity of truth. Gadda's macaronic style is, moreover, a means of deforming reality: a spastic twisting of the real, the effects of which are both alienating and comic.[7] However true and incontrovertible, such assertions tend to overlook how the linguistic and semantic aggregates are held together, what directs the meta-linguistic process, and what is its specific purpose.

In terms of style, the *Pasticciaccio* moves according to what Deleuze calls the 'expliquer-impliquer-compliquer' that form the triad of the fold (1988: 33). First a frame is constructed along conventional narrative

lines, as at the beginning of Chapter 3: 'La mattina dopo i giornali diedero notizia del fatto. Era venerdì' (The next morning the newspapers
reported the event. It was Friday). We have in these two sentences an
announcement of fact: two events made explicit to the reader. In the following two sentences, we are given what is involved in the facts
recorded. The narrator conveys the responses to the commotion, then
describes the terse newspaper report, the style of which deflects the narration onto another register, one devoted to the text of Mussolini and his
regime: 'Ereno passati li tempi belli ... che pe un pizzico ar mandolino
d'una serva a piazza Vittorio, c'era un brodo longo de mezza paggina'
(Gone were th' good ol' days ... when for pinching a maid's ass in
Piazza Vittoria there was a half page of slobbering). This latter twist
in the narration ignites the facts of record, causing them to explode in all
their complexity and implications. One story, the story of the crime,
is linked to another more grievous crime: fascism, which succeeds in
engulfing the narration in numerous satirical folds, all of which are segments of the tangle. If we look closely at the complication, we see that it
has a combustion-like quality. It begins on a note of playful satire:
'Ereno passati i tempi belli [...] La moralizzazione dell'Urbe e de
tutt'Italia insieme, er concetto d'una maggiore austerità civile, si apriva
allora la strada' (Gone were th' good ol' days ... The moralization of the
Urbs and of all Italy, the notion of a strengthened civil austerity, was
then paving the way). Then the pace is quickened and becomes feverish
in the chaotic enumeration of what fascism, through its demagoguery,
pretended it had accomplished:

Delitti e storie sporche ereno scappati via pe sempre da la terra d'Ausonia, come
un brutto insogno che se la squaja. Furti, cortellate, puttanate, ruffianate, rapina,
cocaina, vetriolo, veleno de tossico d'arsenico per acchiappà li sorci, aborti manu
armata, glorie de lenoni e de bari, giovenotti che se fanno pagare er vermutte da
una donna, che ve pare? La divina terra d'ausonia manco s'aricordava più che
robba fusse.(72)

[Crimes and shady stories had fled forever from the land of Ausonia, like a bad
dream goes poof. Pinchings, streetwalking, safe-cracking, flesh peddling, coke,
vitriol, arsenic bought for poisoning rats, shotgun abortions, arabesques of
pimps and cardsharps, youngsters having a lady pay for their drinks, are you
kiddin'? Ausonia's blessed land couldn't remember the meaning of such things.]

From here the connection between the crimes intensifies as it is fixed in the sign of the knife: 'Il coltello, in quegli anni, il vecchio coltello d'ogni maramalduccio e d'ogni guappo 'e malu culori, – o bberbante o ttraddetori, – l'arma de' tortuosi chiasetti, de' pisciosi vicoletti, pareva davvero che fusse sparito di scena pe nun tornacce mai più: salvoché di sulla panza delli eroi funebri, dove si esibiva, ora, estromesso in gloria, come genitale nichelato, argentato' (72–3; The knife, in those years, the old blade of every back stabber, of every two-bit dead-end dick or corner cutthroat, the shivvie of zigzag alleyways and piss-soaked back streets, seemed to have vanished for good from circulation, except on the belly of the heroes lying in state, on which it was now exhibited, unsheathed gloriously, like nickel- or silver-plated genitalia). Stirred up, the narrative now folds out from the world to the subject, Fascism, inflecting itself in a series of possible connections between the crimes, from the Duce to Edda Ciano:

Vigeva ora il vigor nuovo del Mascellone, testa di Morto in bombetta, poi Emiro col fez, e col pennacchio, e la nuova castità della baronessa Malacianca-Fasulli, la nuova legge delle verghe a fascio. Pensare che ci fossero dei ladri, a Roma, ora? Co quer gallinaccio co la faccia fanatica a Palazzo Chigi? Cor Federzoni che voleva carcerà pe forza tutti li storcioni de lungotevere? O quanno se baciucchiaveno ar cinema? Tutti li cani in fregola de la Lungara? Cor Papa milanese e co l'Anno Santo de du anni prima? E co li sposi novelli? Co li polli novelli a scarpinà pe tutta Roma?

Lunghe teorie di nerovestite, affittato er velo nero da cerimonia a Borgo Pio, a piazza Rusticucci, A Borgo Vecchio, si attruppavano sotto ar colonnato, basivano a Porta Angelica, e poi traverso li cancelli de Sant'Anna p'annà a riceve la benedizzione apostolica da Papa Ratti, un milanese de semenza bona de Saronno de quelli tosti, che fabbricava li palazzi. In attesa de venì finarmente incolonnate loro pure: e introdotte dopo quaranta rampe de scale in sala der trono, dar gran Papa alpinista. Pe dì che l'Urbe incarnava omai senza er minimo dubbio la città de li sette candelabri de le sette virtù: quella che avevano auspicata lungo folti millenni tutti i suoi poeti e tutti gli inquisitori, i moralisti e gli utopici, Cola appeso. (Grascio era.) Pe le strade de Roma nun se vedeva più in giro una mignotta, de quelle co la patente. Con gentile pensiero pe l'Anno Santo, il Federzoni le aveva confiscate tutte. La marchesa Lappucelli era a Capri, a Cortina, era annata in Giappone a fa un viaggio.(73)

[Apejaws's (formerly Skull-in-a-derby, then Emir with a fez, and then panache) new force was now in vigour. As was the retouched chastity of the Baroness Malacianca-Fasulli, as was the new law of the fasces. To think that there were thieves in Rome, now! With that fanatic cock-of-the-walk at Chigi palace? And with Federzoni who wanted to clap in jail all the neckers on the Lungotevere? Or when they smooched at the movies? All the mutts in rut down by the river? With that Milanese Pope and the Holy Year of a couple of years ago? With the newlyweds? And the newly hatched chickens chirping all over Rome? Long tiers of black-garbed women with dark ceremonial veils hired at Borgo Pio, in Piazza Rusticucci, in Borgo Vecchio ganged up at the colonnade, went limp at Porta Angelica, then passed through the gates at Sant'Anna to receive the apostolic benediction from Pope Ratti, an uppercrust Milanese from Saronno, the tough kind who gets buildings built: then the ladies waiting to be set up in columns and led, after climbing forty flights of steps, into the throne room of the great Pope Mountaineer. All this, to let us in on the fact that the Eternal City now incarnated, no ifs, ands, or buts, the city of the seven candelabra of the seven virtues: the one invoked, over the caravan of the millennia, by all its poets, its inquisitors, moralists, and utopists, including the hanged Cola (fat as he was). Nary whore (a licensed one) to be seen on the streets of Rome. With heartwarming consideration for the Holy Year, Federzoni confiscated the whole lot. The Marchesa was in Capri, in Cortina, had gone to Japan on a trip.]

To use Deleuze's terminology, the object of narration (fascism) takes on a new status, that of the 'objectile'; it is one and the same with the layers of reference that comprise it: 'Par rapport aux plis dont elle est capable la matière devient matière d'expression' (1988: 52) These folds of matter become expression, however, are not fragments whirling in a void; rather, they are 'derivative forces' originating in the authorial soul and nourished by primitive impulses. Yet the resulting satire is not simply the effect of a personal style, Gadda's stylistic choice, but the reflection of a dynamic within the world itself; its rule of law. Gadda's baroque folds are meant to kill by engulfing the object in a form of destructive purification. Hence we can posit a formal link between Gadda's style and the selected genre of the detective story. It consists in the negative outcome of the latter's positive function of policing society in order to cleanse it of its crimes. If this fails, a case must be made for the power of style to carry out successfully such a function.

Such a passage as the one just cited suggests that for Gadda narration is by its very nature open-ended, for the impulses behind satiric writing, as Jameson has remarked in the case of Wyndham Lewis, can find no 'satisfactory symbolic outlet' (1979: 141); the satiric impulse, in other words, can be checked in a kind of holding operation materialized in ending, but not in concluding, the narration. In marking out his victims,

Gadda, as we shall see in the appendix, projects into the text his own libidinal apparatus which envelops its form. His assault on fascism is at once an act of vengeance and a means of disinculpating the self.

E chi parla e vive, parla e vive necessariamente legato da un complesso di relazioni ambientali e sceniche che lo avviluppano nella totalità delle loro determinazioni [...] Così il dialetto può raggiungere più decisi, più concreti risultati che molte volte una lingua piovutane in penna da una tradizione stenta, da una scuola uggiosa: e, per certe disgraziati, nemmen da quelle. ('Arte del Belli,' *VM*, 560)

[And whoever speaks and lives, speaks and lives connected necessarily to a complex of environmental and place relations which envelop him in the totality of their determinations ... Hence dialect can achieve more decisive and concrete results than often a language derived from a stale tradition and from boring scholastic conventions; and for some unfortunate writers not even from that.]

This statement with which Gadda concludes his essay on the Roman dialect poet G.G. Belli can be usefully summoned as a starting point for any consideration of Gadda's own deployment of dialect, especially in *Quer pasticciaccio*. It posits dialect as a vehicle of the truths embedded in a specific culture which the standard literary language, fettered by tradition and convention, is incapable of capturing. Lest we construe such a statement as a nod in the direction of neo-realism, or as show of solidarity with the proletarian and subproletarian underclass championed by Pasolini, we must locate Gadda's emphasis here in the verb 'avilluppare': whoever lives and speaks in a particular social milieu cannot help being encased in its linguistic signs, in its manner, or manners, of speech. Thus one can account for Gadda's use of dialect in the *Pasticciaccio* in terms of representation as a means of authentic and spontaneous reproduction of a cultural milieu. A host of examples, especially in the interrogation segments, substantiate well such an intention. Take, for instance, Dott. Fumi's questioning of Ines, in which Gadda puts dialect to use for the purpose of conveying the way his characters actually speak. Dott Fumi, who oscillates between Italian and Neapolitan, his native dialect ('"Che cosa faceva Diomede?" Sussultò. "Cos'eran quele donne che ciaveva intorno? Che donne erano?"'), and the uneducated Ines who speaks only Roman dialect.

But the effect of dialect, in this scene as elsewhere, consists much less in its capacity to reproduce real-life speech situations than in the aesthetic, or creative, use to which the qualities of language are put. Between standard and dialect speech there looms the presence of an author-narrator whose principal intention is to exhibit the psychological force of his own language: of how it breaks through convention and artifice to reproduce real speech acts and to mimic them in such a way as to create both comic and tragicomic spectacles. The interrogation scenes in *Quer pasticciaccio* are particularly suited for the staging of the linguistic action and reaction which animates the spectacle. The following is a small segment of the interrogation of Ines Cionini:

Ma gli uomini, quegli uomini, la ricattavano col solo sguardo, acceso e rotto a intervalli, dai segni e dai lampi, non pertinenti alla pratica, di una cupidità ripugnante. Quegli uomini, da lei, volevano udire, sapere. Dietro di loro c'era la giustizzia: na macchina! No strazzio, la giustizzia. Mejo piuttosto la fame; e annà pe strada, e sentisse pioviccicà ne li capelli; mejo addormisse a na panchina de lungotevere, a Prati. Volevano sapere. Mbè? Che cosa trafficava chesto Diomede. E lei zitta. E loro: su su: parlare, cantare [...] 'Che cosa faceva Diomede?' Sussultò [lo Sgranfia]. 'Cos'erano quele donne che ciaveva intorno? Che donne erano?' [...]

Lei, tra l'umiliazzione e la rabbia della gran gelosia che pativa, col volto tuttavia tuffato entro il gomito, co li capelli che spiovevano giù secchi secchi fino al di là del gomito nascondendole del tutto la fronte ... finì pe dì, già, ch'era capace puro d'annà co certe racchie, purché ...

'Purché?'

[...]

'Che arte fa?' domandò il dottor Fumi, con mitezza. 'Che arte facciarìa si nu stesse a spasso?' [...]

'L'ellettricista!' [...]

'Adesso cià d'avé un'ingresa,' affermò riprendendo a singhiozzare in quel fradicio, con infradiciate parole: 'n'americana brutta, cià d'avé, io che ne so? Ma nun è vecchia, questa qui, ma co certi capelli de stoppa!' Si rasciugò il naso nel polsino. 'Cià li sordi, cià. Ecco che cià': e proruppe nuovamente in singhiozzi. 'E cchi è? Vuie 'o sapite, chi è? Dove sta? M' 'o sapisseve dicere? Dite, dite. Chest'americana, quest'inglese ...'

'Che ve pare! Pe chi m'avete preso? Starà là, in quarcuno de queli alberghi de lusso indò ce vanno li signori ...'(170–1)

[But the men, those men, blackmailed her with their gaze alone, afire, broken at intervals by signals and flashes, not pertinent to the case, of a repugnant greed. Those men, from her, wanted to hear, to know. Behind them was Justice: a machine! A torment, that's what Justice was. Hunger was better: and going on the street, and feeling the rain drizzling in your hair: better to go to sleep on a bench by the river, in Prati. They wanted to know. Well? What sort of dealings did this Diomede traffic in? She shut up. And they: come on, come on, talk, spill it [...] 'What did Diomede do?' she started. 'What were those women he had hanging around him? What sort of women were they?' She, between humiliation and the fury of the great jealousy she suffered, her face still plunged into her elbow, her hair falling lankly even behind the elbow, hiding her whole forehead ... ended by saying, sure, he was capable of going even with old bags, as long as they ...

'—As they ?' [...]

'So what does he do?' asked Doctor Fumi, mildly. 'What would his job be, if he wasn't out of work?' [...]

'Electrician!' [...]

'And now he has an English woman,' she stated, resuming her sobs, in that bath, with bathed words: 'an ugly American, he has, but what do I know about it? She isn't old, though, not this one, but with hair like straw!' She wiped her nose on her cuff. 'She has money, that's what she has': and again she burst into sobs. (234–6)]

This orchestration of this dialect sequence is typical in Gadda. The narrator's first glance is from the stance of a relatively detached observer who underlines for the reader the revulsion that he or she should feel in the face of such an outrage. But the violence described heightens the moment of description to a point at which the narrator abandons Italian for what could be the perspective, and thus the dialect thoughts, of the victim ('Mejo piuttosto la fame [...]), hence as Ines tries to free herself from her interlocutors with her lies, so Gadda, in an equally convulsive transition, frees himself from his linguistic norm. We move then to more direct, combative, dialect exchanges between the adversaries. Dott. Fumi's first question ('Che arte fa?') is phrased mildly in Italian, but his exasperation soon escapes the control applied by official speech, which in effect renders his question somewhat vague, so Gadda has him repeat the question in Neapolitan: 'Che arte facciarìa si nu stesse a spasso?' And the more Fumi probes, the more he humbles his victim, the more Gadda has the languages of passion square off against each other in a collision between two reciprocally incomprehensible worlds, of two monads regulated by the intensity of appetite.

In terms of novel form, we can see how Gadda, in his use of dialect, adapts the modernist strategy of conveying individual consciousness from the inside without resorting either to the conventional interior monologue or to the naturalist variants of free indirect discourse. His rendering of the inner reality of his characters amounts to simply transcribing the language in which their appetites are fuelled, that material substratum of consciousness which in moments of heated tension and conflict is impossible to repress. This may, furthermore, be seen as a way of foregrounding the grotesqueness that results from the alienation of human relations, which the normative language tends to conceal.

Gadda's aesthetic, or creative, use of dialect presupposes a self-conscious text and a narrative voice capable not only of perceiving the variables of any given relationship, but also willing to subsume them to the humours of the writing subject, so that what may at first appear as the representation of a dialogical form, geared to secure the reality of the object, as, say, in Belli or Porta, loses all its representational stability in expression. This expressionistic use of dialect then becomes just one other function of the Gaddian baroque in which the object world is intensified at the very same time that it moves in every direction.

Gadda's fierce onslaught on reality in the *Pasticciaccio* which results in the dilation of the object world cannot but have a deep effect on the conception and use of narrative time. The fact that, throughout the novel, Gadda is careful to record the chronological time of the investigation suggests, given the obvious disproportion in relation to the continuously expanding folds of narrative time, that we are dealing with a compensatory structure: an overlay of naturalistic precision ultimately at odds with the existential reality of the narrating subject. To expand the frame of the object to include its infinite articulations and entanglements; this baroque procedure can be viewed as a surrogate for an objectively degraded reality, an attempt to restore some fundamental truth of being to a social milieu ravaged by fascism. What assails the reader as an absolute critique, for its dynamic and prolonged excess, ends up reflecting back on the intellectual posture from which its issues: namely, from Gadda's fundamentally conservative thought manifest in the highly pitched, convulsive tone that masks his intellectual authority. The dispersions and combinations sustained by the novel's narrative, this formidable anxiety behind the quest for expressive space can be most usefully viewed as a symptom of the sense of placelessness animating the Gaddian baroque. As we have already seen, *déclassment*, the main theme of Gadda's biography, can be seen to have a direct effect on the crisis of the individual subject. But here in *Quer pasticciaccio*, unlike in *La cognizione del dolore*, the socio-ideological picture is much more complicated. In the former, the subject's defence of its own position threatened by the popular masses that encroach on its physical and emotional properties is depicted in the full light of the universal value of philosophical thought cast in Gonzalo's would-be reflections on grief and in the melancholy resulting from his sense of dispossession. In *Quer pasticciaccio*, by contrast, we have no narrative subject that sets its claims against a marauding Other; no agent who speaks directly for the narrator/author. Instead, the Other is conceived as a pervasive totality, regulated by its own passions and impulses. It exists alone as prey for the authorial voice to feed upon at will. As the material of satiric production, the novel's degenerated collectivity begs to be cleansed, its fascism castigated, its follies exposed. In so being, the narrative voice displays a kind of schizophrenic quality: while it identifies with Ingravallo's probing philosophic mind, it takes its distance from it, alienating it from itself through the circus mirror of caricature. Such a procedure suggests that for Gadda the satiric violence reserved for Mussolini and his regime can be regarded as a defence mechanism, the attempt to hold at bay his own aggressive fantasies by transforming them into verbal weapons, as well as to compensate for his own involvement in fascism. In this light, the policing of reality serves as a means of unwinding the personal, emotional tension that fuels the narrative engine.

Appendix

Gadda and Fascism

The interview Carlo Emilio Gadda granted to Dacia Maraini in 1968 was meant to leave no doubt whatsoever as to his political sentiment during the years of Fascist rule: 'Solo nel 1934, con la guerra etiopica, ho capito veramente cos'era il fascismo e come mi ripugnasse. Prima non me n'ero mai occupato. Le camicie nere mi davano fastidio e basta [...] Ma solo nel '34, con la guerra etiopica, ho capito veramente cos'era il fascismo. E ne ho avvertito tutto il pericolo'[1] (It was only in 1934 [sic], with the Ethiopian war, that I truly understood what fascism was and how I detested it. Before then I never gave it a thought. The black shirts irked me and that was it ... But only in 1934 I became aware of all the danger). With such a statement, Gadda confirmed what several critics, who were intent on emphasizing Gadda's anti-fascism, wanted to believe: that any possible relationship between Gadda and the regime was limited to a certain patriotic and militaristic rhetoric, attributable to the writer's youth. The enthusiasm with which, in the *Giornale di guerra e di prigionia* and in *Il castello di Udine*, Gadda praised his country, and his inflexible preoccupation with correct military behaviour were, for example, according to Giuliano Manacorda, 'il massimo delle concessioni che Gadda abbia dato al fascismo' (1967: 245; Gadda's greatest concession to fascism). And Adriano Seroni took pains to mark the distinction one must draw between Gadda the nationalist and militarist, and the mature writer who, with the passing of time, realizes the 'anti-historicity' of his youthful vision of things (1969: 93); while, from another perspective, fascism for Gadda was, in the words of Gian Paolo Biasin, something that he experienced and suffered disdainfully in silence ('che egli ha vissuto e sofferto sdegnosamente, silenziosamente' [1968: 473]).

Close examination of Gadda's technical writings from 1931 to 1942 has shown that assessments of Gadda's politics of the kind just cited were in fact ill-founded. Gadda was a 'convinced Fascist,' as Peter Hainsworth has written, who, after the fall of Mussolini and his regime, wrote fierce polemics against fascism. Hainsworth's summation of Gadda's rapport with fascism captures the essence of an experience which will be discussed here:

> Gadda's Fascism was obviously nonconformist, nor was it an incidental or acci-
> dental feature of his experience and work during the *ventennio*. Though he
> might seem now to have been naive or self-deceiving, he clearly saw himself as
> giving measured, thoughtful support to the regime. Fascism responded to his
> need for order and dignity in a world which his own traumatic experience dur-
> ing and after the First World War indicated was bereft of both. (Hainsworth
> 1997: 224)

There is no doubt that fascism's original program contained many elements capable of attracting the disillusioned idealist of the *Giornale di guerra* and *Il castello di Udine*. In its early phases, fascism had presented itself as a reaction against the liberal politics of the moment and the inability of the democratic governments to complete the work of nationalization begun with the Risorgimento. Also, typical of fascism was its contempt for parliamentary government, the same Italian parliament which in Gadda's view was responsible for the badly outfitted troops that lost their lives on the Carso and at Caporetto. Moreover, from a psychological standpoint, surely compatible with fascism are certain character traits manifest in the *Giornale di guerra e prigionia*: namely, Gadda's grandiose sense of his own importance, the endless reiteration of the special character of *his* problems – as, for example, his having to live in an alien world, his fantasies of ideal love, his exhibitionism and self-involvement (his need to place himself always at centre stage) – and, finally, the way he oscillates between indifference and anger, shame and humiliation. So with the *Giornale*, it does not seem that we are dealing with a case of 'vaga retorica giovanile' (vague rhetoric of youth). Instead, Gadda's praise of the fatherland and of genuine and efficient military behaviour, his anti-socialism, and 'anti-giolittismo,' are all to be seen as an expression of the *déclassement* and estrangement of that sector of the liberal-conservative Lombard bourgeoisie to which Gadda belonged and with which he identified. Simply put, Gadda experienced the war as a subject become subordinate in a capitalist society that was extending a friendly hand to the masses. Thus, his deep respect for authority, his consideration of his selfhood as a moral and ethical touchstone, and his tendency to become a passive spectator in a drama of existence; thus the psychopathological contents of the *Giornale*, the continual references made to Gadda's intellectual lethargy, restlessness, spiritual isolation, maladies, boredom, paralysis of the will, all take on a political significance: they express allegorically the drama of a collective subject which attempts to reconstitute itself by means of violent reaction. Only in this sense we can explain the different languages of the *Giornale*, which range from the notable stylization of a Gaddüs, who *'Prospexi Italiam summa sublimis ad unda,'* to expressionist invective and grotesque deformation.

The vision of chaos that Gadda presents in the *Giornale* and in *Il castello di Udine* is integrally narcissistic not so much because it concentrates almost exclusively on the subject in crisis, but rather in that it reproduces the experience of a fragmented self as spectacle (the baroque perspective fundamental to all of Gadda's works). In other words, the 'psychopathology of everyday life' is objectified: disconnected thoughts are reorganized in short narratives, and the effects of danger and desire that they produce supersede decisively the empirical realities related to the actual experience of war. Yet, such a narcissistic disunity, in increasing the force of fragmentation, generates as its own antidote its own terms of order, which are made concrete by the war itself, or better, in the authoritarianism of the moral economy of war. I shall return to the narcissist problematic in evaluating the nature of Gadda's anti-fascism.

The Great War had cut Gadda's ties to the economic stability of his native Milan, which the practical intelligence of his ancestors had moulded into an efficient organism. After the war, emergent fascism succeeded in bringing within its fold the economically disillusioned middle class by offering it the rhetoric of national efficiency, honour, and patriotism, without, however, going beyond the boundaries of traditional politics. There is no doubt, as Cesare Cases had remarked, that Gadda's approach to fascism came from the right: Gadda, a bourgeois engineer, desirous of a functional and well-organized state, could not but be attracted by the authority and pragmatism of Fascist power politics, and, given Gadda's scientific culture and learning, it is not surprising that the aspect of the regime to which he would give priority was its claims to technical efficiency.

Contrary to what Gadda suggests when he states that he had no knowledge of Fascist politics before 1934, there exists a series of articles dating back to 1931, published in the Milanese daily *L'Ambrosiano*, devoted to the characteristics and deployment of light metals and gaseous substances, in which he reveals his support for the autarchic programs then being promoted by the regime. In the first of these articles, entitled 'I metalli leggeri: leghe di magnesio' (2 September 1931), Gadda's favourable attitude towards the regime's economic politics emerges only indirectly. As a matter of fact, five days later (7 September 1931), on the pages of the same newspaper, we find a letter by Arnaldo Mussolini, who, besides praising Gadda's work, exhorts him to venture beyond the purely scientific aspects of his presentation in order to touch upon the economic consequences that might derive from the wide application of light metals. And in the same column, the *Ambrosiano*'s editor is quick to reassure the Duce's brother that Gadda will not disappoint.[2] In fact, Gadda himself, a few pages later, adds the following to his article 'I metalli leggeri':

Le note che seguono avevano già avuto l' accessit dalla Redazione dell'Ambrosiano, allorché l'alto monito del Grand'Ufficiale Dottor Arnaldo Mussolini mi incitò a delineare in modo più netto che non fosse per allusioni e rapidi accenni quei problemi di interesse tipicamente italiano che si riconnettono alla produzione delle leghe leggere ed extra leggere. Conscio che il compito di recare idee definitive spetta ai tecnici specializzati nel ramo, mi farò purtuttavia un grato dovere di attemperami alle direttive segnateci dall'illustre Direttore del Popolo d'Italia.

[The following notes had already been approved by the editorial board of the *Ambrosiano*, when, by lofty admonition, the Great Official Doctor Arnaldo Mussolini encouraged me to delineate in a way other than by allusion and rapid reference those problems of typically Italian interest related to the production of light and extra light metals. Although I am aware that the task of giving precise ideas belongs to the specialists in the field, it will be my pleasure to follow the directives indicated by the Illustrious Director of the Popolo d'Italia.]

In his next article, Gadda in fact describes the beneficial effects of economic autarky:

Arnaldo Mussolini, sensibilissimo interprete della coscienza economica della nazione, ha colto con vigile prontezza il motivo fondamentale del tempo che ci occupa, incuorandoci a conclusioni meno generiche. Egli d'altronde aveva già delineato questo tema e presagito queste conclusioni fin dal 1927, scrivendo che il secolo nostro doveva trovare la sua 'forza' nell'elettricità, la sua materia nei metalli leggeri [...] Se il rifornimento dell'alluminio e del magnesio fosse e dovesse permanere esterno, le loro 'brillanti' applicazioni sarebbero cura dell'ingegnere e del tecnico, ma l'economista e il politico rimarebbero di fronte ad esse in questo stato che Leibnitz chiama 'd'indifferenza' [...] Ma l'alluminio già oggi è totalmente fornito all'Italia dalla industria estrattiva del suo territorio, e in misura già oggi superiore al consumo interno, così che già si affaccia la necessità dell'esportazione o la convenienza di un più largo consumo [...] Applicando leghe leggere ed extraleggere [...] là dovunque è possibile, l'Italia non consegue soltanto una finalità tecnica, ma anche una finalità nazionale in quanto evita di pagare all'estero il diverso metallo che alluminio e magnesio son venuti a sostituire. (1 September 1931)[3]

[Arnaldo Mussolini, a highly sensible judge of the nation's economic pulse, has captured with vigilant alacrity the fundamental problem of our time, encouraging us to consider more precise solutions. He, in fact, had already discussed this theme and proposed the same solutions as far as 1927, writing that our century had to seek its 'force' in electricity, its materials in light metals ... If the supply of aluminum and magnesium is and should remain external, their 'brilliant' application would be the domain of the engineer and technician, and the economist and politician before it would remain in that state that Leibnitz calls 'indifference'... But aluminum is already supplied to Italy from its own mines, and to a degree that its quantity is superior to consumption, so that we already face the need for exportation or for greater internal use ... By putting light and extra light metals to use... where it is possible, Italy not only carries out a technical objective, but also a national objective in that it avoids paying foreign countries the different metals that aluminum and magnesium had come to substitute.]

Moreover, Gadda's interest in economic self-sufficiency is not limited to the articles cited above. Even during the so-called glorious epoch of fascism, he returns to the theme of autarky as consistent with the regime's policy. In 1936, in L'Ambrosiano (in a column entitled 'Orizzonti dell'Impero' [Horizons of the Empire]), Gadda publishes an article entitled 'Risorse minerarie del territorio etiopico,' in which he indicates his approval of the favourable state of mineral research in the newly conquered African colony. His support of the Fascist program appears evident from the opening words: 'La [...] costituzione di un Ente parastatale per le ricerche minerarie in Etiopia [...] è venuta ad esaudire una comune e prima domanda circa l'impostazione del problema e a confermare [...] con quale alacrità il governo fascista, per l'impulso del

Duce, abbia agito in questo senso[4] (The ... creation of a state agency for mineral research in Etiopia ... has responded to a common and essential question regarding the way the problem should be approached, confirming ... the speed with which the Fascist government, through the impulse of Il Duce, has acted in this regard).

In the following year, another series of articles on the same theme appeared in the Turin daily *La Gazzetta del Popolo*,[5] while, in *Le vie d'Italia*, the review of the same Touring Club Italiano that Gadda mocks in *Quer pasticciaccio*,[6] we find more support on Gadda's part for autarky, as for example in 'Le funivie Savona–San Giuseppe di Cairo e la loro funzione autarchica nella economia nazionale.'[7] Yet, although these articles all testify to Gadda's support of the regime's autarkic initiatives, they are, with one exception ('Combustibile italiano'), not in the strict sense 'political'; it would therefore be an exaggeration to accuse Gadda of Fascist complicity on the basis of his support for the government's program of artarcky, which, as it is well known, has it roots in liberal Italy. Moreover, these largely technical writings display – one could   say – a seriousness that is at odds with the facile optimism exhibited by the official scientific culture of the thirties.[8] In truth, if Gadda's acceptance of the national economy were the only instance of cooperation with the regime, it could be regarded simply as a dignified contribution to a then ongoing debate among scientists. But, however true this may be, Gadda, at the same time, was not immune to the vacuous rhetoric and mythical thinking he had sought to combat, as, for example, when he sings the praises of the epic qualities, courage, and enthusiasm of the Fascist youth engaged in the glorious pastime of skiing: 'Tutto è stato arditamente voluto, diligentemente eseguito, perché, raggiunto il cri-nale dell'Italia senza dispendio di tempo, si allegri ognuno delle altissime nevi. Giovini corti bruceranno, nella felice disciplina dello sci, le ore veloci della corsa, le luminose ore di giovinezza' (All has been ardently desired and diligently executed, since, having reached the apex of Italy without loss of time, they all rejoice in the snow-filled peaks. Our young will burn in the joyous discipline of skiing the rapid time of the competition, the luminous hours of their youth).[9]

Moreover, in 1935, we have Gadda's review of General Emilio De Bono's book on the Ethopian war, where, among other things, we read:

La elaborazione della verità storica è, in genere, una cosa complicatissima. Ma il Quadrumviro la raggiunge in questo suo libro con la felice e diretta sicurezza dell'uomo che ha vissuto e combattuto la guerra da bersagliere, cioè nel più rapido, nel più valido modo. Egli ha patito ma soprattutto agito [...] Il libro di Emilio De Bono può considerarsi unico nel suo genere: L'uomo che conduce oggi le operazioni militari nell'Africa parla ai nostri animi 'assetati di cose vere', il linguaggio delizioso della verità, parla, come noi diciamo, 'fuori dai denti', offrendo alla storiografia della guerra un documento che la storiografia stessa [...] non dovrebbe negligere. Troverete nel libro del Quadrumbiro battute che solo dalla penna di un quadrumviro possono venir licenziate 'a buon fine'.

[The elaboration of historical truth is, in general, a complicated matter. But the Quadrumvirate succeeds in doing so in this book with the ease and assurance of someone who has lived and fought as a *bersagliere*, that is, in the quickest and most valiant of ways. He has suffered, but above all has acted ... Emilio De Bono's book can be considered unique: the man who today conducts military operations in Africa speaks to our minds 'thirsty for reality' in the sweet language of truth, he speaks, as we say, 'without mincing words,' providing war historiography a document that historiography itself ... should not ignore. You will find in the Quadrumvirate's book expressions that only a quadrumvirate can sanction with 'noble purpose.']

Finally, the Quadrumvirate is compared to Virgil in a way wholly consistent with the cultural propaganda of the time:

La vita della nazione chiede gran forza ad essere vissuta: e il libro ne fa testimonianza quanto all'autore. Traspare dal turbine una certezza, quella che fu già espressa nei secoli dal poeta di Roma: *Mersit profundo, pulchrior evenit*.

[To live the life of the nation great strength is required. From the storm of war comes a certainty, that which has been already expressed in time by the poet of Rome: *Mersit profundo, pulchrior evenit*.]

After the Fascist war in Africa was successfully concluded, Gadda takes another step in his acceptance of the regime, expressing his trust in Mussolini's foresight and wisdom. In the article 'Combustibile italiano' his praise reaches the limits of hagiography:

Lo spirito mussoliniano, subentrato al brontolamento dell'era liberista anglomane o francomane o che altra fosse, è fede nella validità redentrice dell'azione: nessuno e nulla deve essere disprezzato: tutto e tutti devono essere posti in condizione di adempiere al più alto compito possibile. Come egli porge la mano agli uomini, anche ai diseredati, perché si levino, così tocca le cose perché servino.[10]

[The Mussolinian spirit that has put an end to the confusion of the liberal era (Anglo-manic or Franco-manic or whatever it might have been) means faith in the redemptive validity of action. Nobody and no thing should be scorned; all things and all people must be put in a position to carry out the most serious of possible tasks. As he extends his hand to everyone, even to the disinherited, so that they may rise up, in the same way, he touches things so they may be useful.]

And in the introduction to his essay 'La grande bonificazione ferrarese,' Gadda shows his approval for the government's project with the following words:

Mentre le operanti provvidenze mussoliniane trasformano in terra da lavoro e da frumento le lande impaludate dal cielo o abbandonate dagli uomini, mentre il secolare latifondo siculo è chiamato alla coltivazione intensiva e ferve in tutta Italia, la civile fatica della bonifica e del dissodamento, la nostra Rivista è lieta di potersi allineare in ispirito coi combattenti della grande battaglia.[11]

[While Mussolini's providential work is transforming abandoned swamp-like heaths into arable land fit for growing wheat, while the landed estates of Sicily are have been called to cultivation and the civil labour of reclamation and tillage is resplendent in all of Italy, our Review is happy to join in spirit the combatants of this great battle.]

With Italy's entry into the war, we see no change in Gadda's attitude towards the regime. The highest point in his praise of fascism and Mussolini is reached in 1941 with 'I nuovi borghi della Sicilia rurale,' published in *La Nuova Antologia*, in which Gadda gives indisputable support to the project of 'colonization' of the Sicilian estates:

Lo stato fascista, esprimendo in azione la volontà e le direttive del Duce, ha guardato al latifondo siculo come a problema di bonifica integrale. Le opere necessarie sono riferibili a due competenze: statale e privata: cioè a un ente, lo Stato, che si superordina ai poteri economici e alla capacità giuridica del singolo, apportando al vasto cantiere il suo contributo finanzario di eccezione – attinto da tutta la fede di un popolo – nonché lo strumento del diritto, sotto specie di provvidenza legislativa avente valore di imperio.[12]

[The fascist state, expressing in its deeds the will and directives of Il Duce, has considered the landed estates of Sicily to be a problem of general reclamation.

The necessary work will be carried out in both the private and the public spheres, namely, by an agency, the State, which transcends the economic potential and juridical capacity of the individual, bringing to that vast region an exceptional financial contribution – supported by the faith of an entire people, as well as by the instrument of law under a legislative design having the value of a supreme command.]

And in April 1941, we find in the same review 'I littoriali del lavoro,' in which Gadda lends his support to one of fascism's most acclaimed instituions:

La selezione di cantiere e d'officina è un fatto 'spontaneo', anzi una caratteristica d'ogni attività industriale. Certe ideologie, in certi momenti, parvero contrastarlo: come lesivo [...] agli interessi legati al principio di egualianza. Il cànone egualitario si imputò a difendere la causa d'una bassa capacità generale contro l'emergere dei più atti. Ciò non toglie che la coscienza collettiva, quando è veramente impegnata sull'opera, tenda ad affidarla ai migliori, non ai peggiori [...] La società mussoliniana ha dunque sostituito alla scelta empirica ed istintiva dell'allievo di bottega da parte del vecchio maestro, una scelta o almeno una lode 'nazionale', a perfezionare o ad esprimer le quali adibisce la totalità sistemata delle sue energie di lavoro, dei suoi ordinamenti politici [...] Tutta la Nazione Madre assiste al certame dei figli [...] compiacendosi d'un empito giovane, che si libera e si richiude nel disegno della gara. I littoriali sembrano riportare alla collettività militante il compito anticamente assolto da ogni maestro d'arte nell'oscura bottega: predispone il lavoro del domani; le braccia e gli animi del domani.[13]

[The choice of a yard or workshop is a natural one, indeed it is a characteristic of all industrial activity. Certain ideologies at times appear to take issue with it as harmful ... to the interests that rely on the principle of equality. The egalitarian canon is summoned to defend the cause of the little capacity of the masses against the more capable. This does not exclude that the collective consciousness, when it is truly committed to an end, tends to assign the task to the best, not the worst ... Mussolinian society has therefore supplanted the empirical and instinctual choice of the apprentice who acts in behalf of his master with a choice or at least with a 'national' praise, sustained by the work energy and political orientation of an organized totality ... The entire Mother Nation participates in the combat of its children ... taking pleasure in the youthful zeal that both liberates and encloses itself in the rules of the game. The littoriali appear to pass on to the militant collectivity the task traditionally carried out in the dimly lit shop of every artisan: it presupposes the work of the future; the strength and the spirit of the future.]

Finally, in the same article, we have what would appear to be the most un Gaddian of all of Gadda's Fascist advocacy: his praise for the Fascist health ideals:

La concezione del modello-uomo che le dottrine mussoliniane ci presentano, eguagliando e superando la romana e la latina, postula una cospirazione armoniosa delle facoltà naturali: esclude che il Littore dell'arte propria debba venire salutato un giovane difettoso nei muscoli, ginnicamente incapace. Esclude del pari che il vigore e l'abilità del braccio, della mano, siano retti da un animo assolutamente inconscio dei compiti civili demandati ad ogni uomo: dei vincoli, poi, che avvincono ogni opera, ogni pragma, ai modi e ai principi del sapere.[14]

[The conception of the perfect man that Mussolini's doctrines present is equal to and supersedes its Roman and Latin models. It postulates an harmonious blend of natural faculties, excluding that a Littore of his own art can ever be lacking in muscle, athletically incapable. It also rules out that the vigour and capacity of one's arm and hand may be sustained by a mind absolutely unconscious of the civil tasks demanded of every man: of the connections that link every job, every practice, to the means and principles of knowledge.]

Even in 1942, when many were beginning to reject the rhetoric of Mussolini's war policy, Gadda continues to write articles insensible to the reality of Italy's position in the war. While the morale of Fascist Italy was virtually destroyed by bombardments, hunger, and governmental purges, Gadda is praising the cultural and political heritage of ancient Rome and the important mission of the then founded Istituto di Studi Romani.[15]

Only in 1943 it may be possible to detect a light ironic tone in Gadda's journalism. The article 'All'insegna dell'alta cultura,' for example, appears to betray a somewhat different attitude towards a Fascist cultural institution. Following the preceding article on the Istituto di Studi Romani, Gadda describes the activities of the institute of high culture in Milan, but here his language and style show considerably less enthusiasm for the Fascist claim to cultural primacy and the spiritual mission of the Latin race. By means of metaphors bordering on the grotesque, such as 'i focolari del sapere' (fireplaces of knowledge) where 'si afforna pane per lo spirito' (bread for the spirit is cooked) or his description of the workings of the Milanese institute as 'un irradiare di postiglioni al galoppo del castello del principe, su tutte le raggere delle strade, verso lontane missioni' (a radiation of messengers from the prince's castle over a whole network of roads towards distant missions), where the reference to 'postiglioni' (ancient mail-carriers) suggests also uniforms with large metallic buttons, Gadda seems to be parodying the epic style of Fascist propaganda he himself deployed in many of the articles cited above. Moreover, his change of attitude is also apparent in his use of inverted commas around certain official Fascist words and phrases, such as 'cicli culturali,' 'Secolo XX,' 'mens contemporanea,' a practice that appears to convey sarcasm. Finally, the allusively ironic style of a number of passages is reminiscent of some of his early narratives in which the narrator's enthusiasm for the objects described becomes a means of grotesque representation. For example, in reference to the Codex Squarcialupi recently acquired by the institute, Gadda writes:

Vidi, vidi, questo alluminato codice membranaceo degli anni danteschi, fogli d'una pergamena che dava brividi alla palpitazione, d'una morbidezza vellutata, vivente, quasi la stupenda pelle d'un essere appartenente a un quarto regno della natura, o della storia [...] Nella stessa arca, ch'è cava segreta, profonda, irraggiungibile dalle mani dell'acqua, soggiacente ai primi livelli idrici del ghiaione milanese palpitai d'amorosa venerazione davanti il manoscritto originale [...][16]

[I saw, I saw, this illuminated, membranal codex of Dante's time, parchment leaves that made one shiver at the touch, velvety soft, lifelike, like the stupendous skin of some being belonging to the fourth realm of nature or of history ... In the same arc, which is a secret cave, distant from water's hands, deep under the Milanese gravel beneath the first water levels my heart fluttered with amorous veneration before the original manuscript ...]

As we have seen, only in 1937, with 'Combustibile italiano,' does Gadda's praise of fascism take on a mythical quality. Before then, apart from the enthusiasm he demonstrates for General De Bono and the young skiers atop the Gran Sasso, Gadda is careful not to contaminate the rational-technological motivation behind his writings. We could then suppose that he remained essentially undecided or sceptical, as an estranged conservative to the right of the mainstream of fascism, identifying from time to time, but always with some degree of detachment, with the regime's technical projects which, he believed, promised a decisive improvement in the Italian economy.

If we look at the early literary works, we see that Gadda's attitude with respect to his own bourgeois class was problematic. He positioned himself on its perimeter, mocking its vacuous rituals and lack of ideals, while his conservative beliefs made it impossible for him to imagine a different kind of society; thus, the continual friction with a world that could not be, expressed in his well-known expressionistic outbursts and contemptuous invectives, fed his own eccentricity. Gadda's sense of a fragmented existence and his tendency to see himself as part of wholly negative totality become the terms of a dialectic within his Gadda-like characters, a dialectic that is never resolved, nor transcended. The time suspended in *reverie* is counterbalanced by the strong material presence of the corruptibility and real historicity of the world. Therefore, Gadda's literary texts demonstrate, as we have seen, the ongoing, unresolved dilemma of negation of and subjection to the power of the Other. To vindicate this state of ambivalence, Gadda unleashes his linguistic attack, his revolution, which discloses at once the will to penetrate the phenomenal world and to bring it to the same state of extreme crisis that absorbs the narrating subject.

Where then in this picture do we situate Gadda's fascism? Is it possible to reconcile two apparently contrasting ideologies: one which informs Gadda's technical writings through 1942, and the language of Gaddian narrative, particularly of *La cognizione del dolore*, which was serialized in *Letteratura* during the same period? And, given the real existence of a Fascist Gadda, how then do we account for his vitriolic anti-fascism?

First of all, it is useful to note the instances of praise for Mussolini and Fascist institutions that we find within Gadda's technical writings are mainly ceremonial formulas. Expressions like 'lo spirito mussoliniano,' 'le operanti provvidenze mussoliniane,' 'la Nazione Madre,' derive from the need to behave and respect the rules of etiquette which prescribe that one says what the other wants to hear.[17] This, of course, does not mean that Gadda was not a believer: if not precisely in fascism, he certainly believed in the need to participate from time to time in the cultural habits of the dominant group, that is, in the authoritarian apparatus from which he felt deeply alienated. This respect for authority, linked to his feeling of being different, is what leads him to participate passively, that is, narcissistically, in the spectacle of power, emitting those propagandistic slogans designed to produce orgiastic pleasure in the listener.

Moreover, Gadda's celebration of fascism was no doubt affected by his experience as a Milanese conservative whose class privileges and security had become unstable with the rise of the petty bourgeoisie to positions of prestige and influence. For Gadda, who saw himself suspended in a fragmented, insecure world, fascism represented order and direction, its program of autarky and myths of national independence seemed to resurrect the dead ideals of his illustrious, enterprising forebears. These general circumstances are in turn conditioned by private experiences that bear upon his class reality in such a way as to constitute principal referential nuclei, as, for example, the violent death in the First World War of his younger brother Enrico and, more important, the imprudent financial investments of his father relative to the construction of a villa in Longone and the cultivation of silkworms. Gadda's anti-fascism is linked in large measure to this latter experience, which becomes in effect his contempt for the petty bourgeois and popular elements of the ruling class seen for the most part as provincial and semi-literate. As a matter of fact, the attack Gadda mounts against Mussolini and Fascism in *Quer pasticciaccio* and *Eros e Priapo* comes from the right, from that same base which led him to extol what he regarded as the regime's economic efficiency and enterprising spirit. Paradoxically, it is, to a large degree, an attack against the narcissistic impulses present in his anti-democratic and pro-fascist sentiment.

Hence Gadda's anti-fascist invectives and satire are tightly bound to his conservative base and can in no way be regarded as the expression of hidden, or repressed, democratic sentiments. Peter Hainsworth's recent essay on Gadda and fascism, while mindful of the psychological complexity of Gadda's anti-Fascist verbal aggression, is careful not to ignore its reactionary and even racist inflections. There is little need to return to what is now very familiar ground. Nevertheless, it may be still useful to point out that Gadda's 'political' texts, as it were, are to be read very much in the same way as his fiction, that is, as a narrative technique which consists in the creative control of the narrator's own obsessions, of thoughts about self which, as Pasolini has observed, are to be negated because they characterize unacceptable modes of behaviour.[18] Thus writing for Gadda is a means of distracting himself from the insidious thoughts he is incapable of repressing, which repeatedly burst into consciousness. What derives from it is a semantics of anxiety manifest in the compulsive linguistic ritual of description. Gadda's descriptive approach reveals his incapacity to concentrate on one specific object or objective – a defect, Lacan would say, in the mechanism of desire. From the standpoint of readers accustomed to ordering formal associations in such a way to indicate the object to which they refer, Gadda's syntax exhibits an infraction of logical coherence because it forms associations only on the basis of internal, pre-textual referents that demand to be included in the narration, but are censured (yet not cancelled) precisely at the moment when their presence is felt. The internal dynamics of such a state are then expressed through an obsessive verbal reaction. The obsession generates a spontaneous reaction that serves as a means of controlling that obsession, replacing the empirical reality of the stimulus. In other words, the description removes the reader's attention from the object at the very same time it underlines its eternal presence. It appears as a kind exorcism of the overbearing presence of a reality that cannot be driven out of consciousness, but only continually dismantled and reinvented. The free association that, in *La cognizione del dolore*, transforms the bells into enormous, monstrous penises which ejaculate their sound on the rich, green countryside is the same that transforms Mussolini, in *Eros e Priapo*, into a satiric object of the first magnitude. The target is pathological narcissism; culturally speaking, the Nietzschean process of ego inflation that becomes psychopathological delusion. But Gadda overturns the Nietzschean psychological model: his invective against the grandiose inflation of the self acts as a screen against those very delusions and fantasies from which his hysterical style derives. The will to power, in other words, has been rejected by the consciousness of a declassed and guilt-ridden subject, paradoxically by the same subject whose *déclassement* generates that very will to subvert. If Gadda, in the person of Gonzalo Pirobutirro, deserves and bears full responsibility for everything that happens to him, and if he is capable, as Gonzalo is, of being one with himself and, at the same time, with the voice that inflicts on him the most impersonal and hostile of judgments, then it is not hard to understand the dynamics at play in Gadda's anti-Fascist diatribes, especially in *Eros e Priapo*. Guido Lucchini is perfectly right in stating that 'the portrait of the "mad narcissist" [Gadda] sketches in *Eros e Priapo* [...] does not stand out either for depth or originality' (1997: 182).

What Lucchini misses, however, is that, in spite of its theoretical weaknesses, the polemic against narcissism in *Eros e Priapo* is very effective if viewed as a kind of exorcism, as satire levelled against the self, that is, against that inclination within the victimized self to want to run with the pack, to gain back some of the celebrity lost in a dreary, commonplace world; put another way, to exhibit the solitary self and, in so doing, take revenge on history. For this reason, the same Mussolini praised in the technical articles cited above reappears in the pamphlet not only as the perpetrator of a civil and political tragedy, but as the grotesque embodiment of unleashed psychic forces, Eros being the aggregate of vital instincts directed towards copulation with and subjection to the tyrant, while Priapo referring to the Duce's perverse exhibitionism. In *Eros e Priapo*, Gadda devotes his satiric energy to elaborating a prolonged metaphor of collective rape: Mussolini has subverted the natural rhythm of human development and from his person emanate rays of narcissistic energy that testify to the eternal presence of the auto-erotic phase of his psyche. The Duce, in fact, appears as a gigantic phallus ready to deflower a world of victims predisposed to the violence of his seductive rhetoric:

Porgeva egli alla moltitudine l'ordito della sua incontinenza buccale, ed ella vi metteva spola di clamori, e di folli gridi, secondo ritmi concitati e turpissimi [...] La moltitudine, che al dire di messer Nicolò amora, la è femmina, e femmina a certi momenti nottivaga, simulava a quegli ululati l'amore e l'amoroso delirio [...]

E al mezzo [...] lo sporgimento di quel suo prolassato e incinturato ventrone, in dondolamento ad avanti-indietro, da punte a tacchi, irrigiditi i ginocchi, di quel mappamondo suo goffo e inappetibile a qualunque. Indi la reiterata esultazione di tutto il corpo, come lo iscagliasse ad alto una molla, e di tutta la generosa persona [...] indi poi chella fulgurata protuberazione di chella proboscide fallica, e grifomorfa in dimensione suina, che dall'abundanzia di carne dell'apparato buccinatorio e del buccale sfinctere e labiale bucco gli era con tutto giolitto e deiezione patria d'ogni disceso de'Malfrullati assentita.[19]

[He set before the multitude the tangled deceptions of his incontinent orifice, and the multitude responded with their clamoring, and with frenzied outbursts, to the beat of the most indecent and agitated rhythms ... The multitude, which according to the bitter saying of Messer Nicolò, is a woman, and a woman at certain moments wanders in the night, would, with its ululations, simulate love and the delirium of love's embrace ...

And in the middle, at the center of the pantomime ... the bulge of that fat, prolapsed belly wrapped in its belt, rocking back and forth, from toes to heels, stiff at the knees, that globe shaped paunch of his, clumsy and repulsive to anyone. Thus the reiterated exultation of the whole body, as if it were being thrust up high by a spring, and of the whole bloated persona ... and so then the dazzling protuberance of that phallic and snout-shaped proboscis of his, the size of a pig's, which through the fleshiness of its bugling apparatus and of the lips and sphincter of its orifice, he was pleasantly at peace with everything, and the fatherland's defecation of every descendent of the Evil- blends in consent.][20]

The metaphor reaches its climax in the transfer of spermatic and seminal force from the sexual organs to Mussolini's virulent rhetoric which he ejaculates on the heads of his worshippers.

Eretto ne lo spasmo su zoccoli tripli [...] il somaro dalle gambe a icchese aveva gittato a Pennino ed ad Alpe il suo raglio. Ed Alpe e Pennino echeggiarlo, hì-hà, hì-hà, riecheggiarlo infinitamenti hè-jà, hè-jà, per infinito cammino de le valli [...] a ciò che tutti, tutti!, i quarantaquattro millioni della malorsega, lo s'infilassero ognuno nella camera timpanica dell'orecchio suo, satisfatto e pagato in ogni sua prurigo, edulcorato, inlinito, imburrato, imbesciamellato, e beato. (*EP*, 243)

[Erect in its spasm upon triple-high hoofs ... the knock-kneed donkey had flung its braying to the Apennines and to the Alps. And Alps and Apennines to echo and re-echo it endlessly, hee-haw, hee-haw, through the endless windings of their valleys ... so that everyone, every single one! The forty-four million participants in this disgrace, might each stick it into the tympanic chamber of his ear, and have their every itch and desire satisfied and fulfilled, sweetened, smeared with ointment, buttered all over, covered in béchamel, and beatified.]

In giving full rein to his satiric impulse, Gadda maintains he has written the history of a generation 'grown old in silence' ('Per "silentium ad senectutem"'), while at the same time confessing that his vigorous opposition to every form of narcissism motivates 'una attitudine critica e una costante beffa della scemenza, ivi compresa la sua propria' (*QP*, 328; a critical attitude and a constant mockery of idiocy, including his own). Hence criticism has justifiably attributed to Gadda's anti-fascism a distinctly meta-historical significance: Gadda's assault on the figure of Mussolini is a means of representing the non-sublimated erotic–narcissist impulse, the roots of which are to be found in the pulsations of an ego genetically contaminated by the id.

It goes without saying that Gadda's anti-Fascist invectives are essentially conservative or reactionary in nature in that they take as their object of ridicule sex and desire, not to mention Woman, the principal culprit:

Non nego alla femina il diritto ch'ella 'prediliga li giovani, come quelli che sono li più feroci' (Machiavelli, *Il Principe*) cioè i più aggressivi sessualmente; ciò è suo diritto e anzi dirò suo dovere. Non nego che la Patria chieda alle femine di adempiere al loro dovere verso la Patria che è, soprattutto, quello di lasciarsi fottere. E con larghezza di vedute. Ma "li giovini" se li portino a letto e non pretendano acclamarli prefetti e ministri alla direzione d'un paese. E poi la femina adempia ai suoi obblighi e alle sue inclinazioni e non stia a rompere le tasche con codesta ninfomania politica, che è cosa ìnzita. La politica non è fatta per la vagina: per la vagina c'è il su' tampone appositamente conformato per lei dall'Eterno Fattore e l'è il toccasana dei toccasana; quando non è impestato, s'intende. Talune gorgheggiavano e nitrivano gargarizzandosi istericamente di 'Patria', talaltre di 'inghilterra deve scontare i suoi delitti'. (*EP*, 245–6)

I do not deny women the right to 'prefer young men, since those are the most ferocious' (Machiavelli, *Il Principe*), in other words, the most sexually aggressive; that is their right, and indeed, their duty. Nor do I deny that women are asked to fulfil their duty to the Fatherland which is, above all, that of letting themselves be fucked. And to be broadminded about it. So let 'young men' be taken to bed, but don't try to promote them as the prefects and ministers in charge of a country. And then women may fulfil their obligations and follow their inclinations, and not be breaking our balls with this political nymphomania, which is something impure. Politics is not made for the vagina: for the vagina there is the tampon, which is appropriately shaped for it by the Eternal Maker, and is the vagina's cure-all of cure-alls; as long as the tampon is not already used, of course. Some of the women would warble and neigh, gargling hysterically with invocations of 'Fatherland'; others with 'England must pay for its crimes.']

The pathological narcissism Gadda satirizes in *Eros e Priapo* can be viewed as a metaphor for contemporary mass culture, which was heralded by the Fascist system of cultural communication. The displacement of traditional modes of collective life facilitates the mass communication which the people automatically consume. Consumption then becomes the primary social relation and the sign of a culture that has taken the place of traditional values: a culture founded on the production of words. To the Gaddian isolated self the words of political propaganda, like the word of God, represent a universal image. The contingency of the self Gadda celebrates throughout his works finds in fascism compensation in the unity of the object of consumption, that is, 'Il Duce,' 'La Patria,' 'La Razza,' and so on.

Eros e Priapo may be thought of, therefore, as an attempt to exorcize the demon potentially present in the solitary self. In telling the story of the phallus's will to power, it captures all the symptoms present in the process of possession, while at the same time making possible the narrator's refuge from contamination behind the mechanism of the pastiche. With the development of capitalism, mass culture becomes ever more consolidated and coordinated. Modern managerial systems depend on the existence of a professional elite in which the highest levels of society come together. This brings about an even greater fragmentation of the masses, which, however, is overcome by a form of communication that urges the people to reorganize for the good of the community. The atomized self, in other words, becomes the vehicle that guarantees conformity. This consumerist narcissism (the unity of self within a general conformity) is augmented by the movement of the masses towards war. It is here that Gadda's reactionary polemic wilfully contradicts the forces of political reaction. By mocking the dynamics of coercion, which has mustered all of its adulatory resources in order to homogenize a culturally diverse people, Gadda insists, with tragic irony, that the reunification will take place in the timelessness of the eternal: *da furore a cenere.*

Notes

Preface

1 Gadda's rise to prominence can be charted along different tracks of critical interest, all of which have emphasized the extraordinary force of his language and style. The significance of his work lies in very much the satirical attitude of mind common to such writers as Musil, Broch, and Céline, while the lyrical and expressive features of his prose, it is generally agreed, reach heights equalled only by Proust and Joyce. What sets him apart from his Italian contemporaries is a ruthless scepticism which breeds forms of satire and pastiche geared to dissolve all forms of metaphysical and historical certainty into fiction, play, and spectacle. The destabilizing power of his prose has changed the course of the Italian novel in our time. The naturalist and neo-realist traditions his writings undermine have now all but disappeared, their realities crushed under the creative yoke of his parody and satire. For an introduction to Gadda, the man and writer, as well as to the range and complexity of his work, see Bertone and Dombroski, eds., 1997.
2 For a complete discussion of these themes, see Maravall 1986, and Bryan S. Turner's introduction to Buci-Glucksmann 1994. On the subject of Gadda and the baroque, see Raimondi 1990 and Manganaro 1994. The perspectives taken in these studies are different but not incompatible with the one taken here.
3 Jenck's formulation is based largely on the concept of 'cosmogenesis' used by the astrophysicist David Layzer (1990).

1: Gadda and the Baroque

1 *I viaggi la morte*, in Gadda, *Saggi Giornali Favole I*, ed. Dante Isella (1991: 434, 496). Hereinafter cited in the text as *VM*.

2 See *Il castello di Udine*, in Gadda, *Romanzi e Racconti I*, ed. Dante Isella (1989: 119–22). Hereinafter cited in the text as *CU*.

3 *La cognizione del dolore*, in ibid, 760. Hereinafter cited in the text as *CD*.

4 In the case of the Spanish baroque, with 'a seigneural, Catholic ruling class that needs to differentiate itself from the sordid world of commerce and manual labor' (Beverley 1993: 59).

5 A concept of the neo-baroque has also been developed by Omar Calabrese (1992) as an effective substitute for the term 'postmodernism.' In Calabrese's view, the neo-baroque refers to the recurrence in contemporary art and culture of forms that recall the historical baroque. Calabrese is careful not to impugn the specificity of the historical moment or the singular case, factors that condition the expression of either the baroque or the classical formal constant. At the same time, his rigorously formalistic procedure focuses exclusively on the text's underlying morphologies. Calabrese's approach has a particular relevance for Gadda in that it theorizes the baroque as a modern cultural and literary trope. Moreover, by considering the baroque as a cultural system displaying specific formal characteristics, Calabrese's discussions place us squarely within Gadda's own referential arena. As regards postmodernism, Gadda's use of parody and citation have no doubt something in common with postmodern literary practices, but his ongoing fascination with the depth and difficulty of his subject matter and with a hermeneutic based on cognition, investigation, and decipherment sets his work apart from postmodernism's most important constitutive features.

6 The formative influence of Leibniz on Gadda can be attested to in the *Meditazione milanese* and by Gadda's choice to write his doctoral thesis on Leibniz's theory of knowledge in the *Nouveaux essais*, a study he never completed.

7 Gadda, *Acquainted with Grief*, translated by William Weaver (1969: 3–4). Hereinafter cited in the text as *AG*.

8 The presence, stylistic and otherwise, of Manzoni in Gadda's fiction is extensive. Gadda sensed – I think rightly – a certain fascination on Manzoni's part for the baroque. On Manzoni and the baroque, see Mazzotta 1989.

9 See Italo Calvino's introduction to *That Awful Mess on Via Merulana*, v.

10 On the novel's title, see Manzotti 1996. Manzotti argues most convincingly that Gadda took his title directly from Schopenhauer's *The World as Will and Representation*, which he read in Italian translation. Manzotti's discussion of the novel's title is the most thorough to date.

11 *Quer pasticciaccio brutto de via Merulana*, in Gadda, *Romanzi e Racconti II*, ed. Dante Isella (1989: 16). Hereinafter cited in the text as *QP*.

12 Gadda, *That Awful Mess on Via Merulana*, translated by William Weaver (1985: 5. Hereinafter cited in the text as *AM*.

13 See Calvino's perceptive remarks in *Six Memos for the Next Millennium*: '[In Gadda's novels] the least thing is seen as the center of a network of relationships that the writer cannot restrain himself from following, multiplying the details so that his descriptions and digressions become infinite. Whatever the starting point, the matter in hand spreads out, encompassing ever vaster horizons, and if it were permitted to go on further and further in every direction, it would end by embracing the entire universe' (107).

14 In Italian literature, such a category would include writers as different from one another as Alfieri and Svevo. The constitution of the subject of narrative and its functions in the history of Italian narrative fiction up to Gadda remains essentially the same in that it is based on the premise that the purpose of narration is to give unity and thus to resolve the contradictions in the social order from which the fiction ultimately derives.

15 On the knot and the labyrinth as baroque figures, see Calabrese 1992: 131–43.

16 '*Every perception is hallucinatory because perception has no object*. Conscious perception has no object and does not refer to a physical mechanism of excitation that could explain it from without: it refers only to the exclusively physical mechanism of differential relations among unconscious perceptions that are comprising it within the monad. And unconscious perceptions have no object and do not refer to physical things. They are only related to the cosmological and metaphysical mechanism according to which the world does not exist outside of the monads that are conveying it' (Deleuze 1993: 93–4).

2: Baroque Solitude; Disillusion and the Ruins of War

1 *Giornale di guerra e di prigionia*, in Gadda, *Saggi Giornali Favole II*, ed. Dante Isella (1992: 431–867). Hereinafter cited in the text as *GGP*.

2 Gadda 1993a: 124.

3 On the close relationship between the *Castello* and the *Giornale*, see Raffaella Rodondi's commentary on *Il castello di Udine*, in Gadda, *Romanzi e racconti I*, ed. Raffaella Rodondi, Guido Lucchini, and Emilio Manzotti (1988: 803–27).

4 'Sono le balaustrate del Luxembourg, dolci e malinconiche in un mattino d'ottobre, e quelle che simmetrizzano le terrazze e i jet d'eau di Versailles, e quelle, fastigi marmorei, dei ponti: sotto cui passa il buon fiume borghese della vecchia patria, della patria reale e storica; che non si può dimenticare, che non si dimentica mai [...] fino a quando alcunché di umano vige nell'animo nostro' (*VM*, 579; The balustrades of Luxembourg, sweet and melancholic on an October morning, and those that give symmetry to the ter-

races and the *jet d'eau* of Versailles, and those, marble pinnacles, of the bridges under which runs the friendly bourgeois river of our ancient fatherland, the real and historical fatherland that cannot be forgotten, that will not be forgotten … as long as a spark of humanity remains in our spirit).

5 In *Castello* such a moral opposition is clearly stated: 'Sono disceso, con la sensazione e con il pensiero, a guardare "le conseguenze del mio interventismo". Sono disceso. Ma sono risalito poi sempre nella solitudine mia, mentre il codazzo delle contumelie che inseguiva i "volontari"e gli "interventisti"faceva gazzarra e stormo fuor de'miei timpani, come la plebaglia fuori di un castello munito. Vigili angosce dominarono la mia guerra, nonostante il bere, il mangiare, il concupire vanamente e il ristoro de'pediluvi: soffrii per gli altri e per me, teso con tutti i nervi nella speranza, e quasi in una continua preghiera. Vigili angosce dominarono la mia guerra, una cieca e vera passione, fatta forse (giudicandola dal punto di vista della raffinatezza italiana) di brutalità, di bestialità, di retorica e di cretinismo: ma fu comunque una disciplina vissuta, la sola degna di esser vissuta' (136; I came as far as to consider, emotionally and rationally, 'the consequences of my interventionism.' I went as far as that. But then I returned as always to my solitude, while the roar of insults which followed the 'volunteers' and the 'interventionists' assailed my ears, like the rabble yelling outside of a fortified castle. A vigilant anguish took hold of my war, despite the drinking, eating, vacuous sex, and the relief of foot baths. I suffered for the others and for me, nervously hoping and almost continually in prayer. A vigilant anguish took hold of my war, a blind and authentic passion, consisting (to judge it by the standards of Italian refinement) of brutality, brutishness, rhetoric, and idiocy. It was nevertheless a lived discipline, the only discipline worth living).

6 Cf. Sokel 1959: 55.

7 See Buci-Glucksmann 1994: 140.

8 Benjamin 1985: 33. See also Buci-Glucksmann 1994: 155.

9 On 'Dott. Feo Averrois,' see Manuela Bertone's excellent analysis (1993: 72–83).

3: Creative Bodies: Theory And Practice of the Grotesque

1 Gadda, *Meditazione milanese*, in *Scritti vari e postumi*, ed. Dante Isella, (1993b: 615–894). Hereinafter cited in the text as *MM*.

2 Piero Martinetti (1872–1934) taught theoretical philosophy at the University of Milan until 1931, when he was forced to leave his Chair for not having sworn allegiance to fascism. In opposition to Croce and Gentile, Martinetti's

idealism, which incorporated the findings of science, was a sort of 'empirical metaphysics' aimed at establishing the unity of all empirical knowledge. The influence of Martinetti on Gadda is mostly limited to the role played by metaphysics in the cognitive process. 'Nessun pensiero è possibile se non in quanto si inquadra in una concezione metafisica (Martinetti 1904: 8; No thought is possible less it is framed by a metaphysical conception) is echoed in Gadda's reflection on his own poetic: 'Quando scriverò la Poetica, dovrà ognuno che si proponga di intenderla, rifarsi dal leggere l'Etica: e anzi la Poetica sarà poco più che un capitolo dell'Etica: e questa deriverà dalla Metafisica' (When I write my Poetics, anyone who hopes to understand it, must read my Ethics: the Poetics is actually nothing more than a chapter of the Ethics, and the latter derives from the Metaphysics; 'Meditazione breve circa il dire e il fare' [in *VM*, 444]).

3 On this point, see Gian Carlo Roscioni's introduction to the first published edition of *Meditazione milanese*, ed. Gian Carlo Roscioni (Turin: Einaudi, 1974), xxv–xxvii.

4 Ibid, xi.

5 With particular reference to the *Pasticciaccio*, it has been noted that the novel can be read in light of the theoretical hypotheses Gadda elaborated in the years between the *Racconto italiano di ignoto del Novecento* (1924) and the *Meditazione milanese* (1928). See Amigoni 1995: 26.

6 I use these terms to indicate the different linguistic registers present in Gadda's work rather than the creation of a variety of voices different from his own. In the last analysis, the authorial voice pervades Gadda's texts at every level, leaving no room whatsoever for the intrusion of feelings, emotions, and thoughts that are not its own, at least to some degree.

7 *Meditazione milanese*, in Gadda, *Scritti vari e postumi*, ed. Dante Isella (1993b: 628). Hereinafter cited in the text as *MM*.

8 See Roscioni's discussion of Gadda and Saussure in his introduction to *Meditazione milanese*, vii–xi.

9 *Racconto italiano di ignoto del Novecento (Cahier d'études)*, in Gadda, *Scritti vari e postumi*, ed. Dante Isella (1993b: 381–613). Hereinafter cited in the text as *RI*.

10 Gadda writes in his note to the passage: 'Giorgio De Chirico ha parodiato con senso d'ironia e di profonda poesia il noto quadro di Böcklin; che dicesi ispirato da uno strapiombo sul mare, a Corfù, coronato di cipressi: incurvi questi nel vento' (*CU*, 217; Giorgio De Chirico parodied with a sense of irony and of profound poetry Böcklin's famous painting; which, it is said, was inspired by a sea cliff at Corfu crowned with cypresses bowing in the wind). And elsewhere, in another note glossing his mention of De Chirico, he remarks: 'Giorgio De Chirico, pittore francamente ammirato dal Ns., ha tutta

una serie di tele Egeo-archeologiche, occupate da certi cavalli sui generis, che a Firenze li chiamano 'i'avallini di De Chirico' (CU, 280; Giorgio De Chirico, a painter frankly admired by the author, has a whole series of Aegean-archaeological canvases, populated by certain horses *sui generis*, which in Florence are called De Chirico's 'avallini'). For a complete discussion of Gadda and De Chirico, see Lipparini 1984: 109–26.

11 Consider for example the episode of the bread riots in Milan. The narrator's grotesque description of the woman fleeing the city ('pancione smisurato, che pareva tenuto a fatica da due braccia piegate: come una pentolaccia a due manichi; e di sotto a quel pancione uscivan due gambe, nude fin sopra il ginocchio, che venivano innanzi barcolando ...' (Her arms were curved under the enormous mass of her belly, and seemed scarcely able to hold it up; it looked like a great earthenware jar with two handles. Below that belly came a pair of legs, naked to above the knee, and staggering unsteadily forward) maintains some degree of objective consistency in relation to the scene, that is, to the distortion she afflicts upon herself in attempting to run holding in her skirt a great quantity of flour: *I promessi sposi*, ed. Lanfranco Caretti (1966: 192); *The Betrothed*, translated by Bruce Penman (1972: 228).

12 For a comprehensive account of Gaddian satire, see Sbragia 1996.

13 Jameson 1979: 140.

14 *Anastomòsi*, in Gadda, *Saggi Giornali Favole I*, ed. Dante Isella (1991: 338).Hereinafter cited in the text as *AN*.

15 In his annotated edition of the novel (Turin: Einaudi, 1987), Emilio Manzotti reminds us of similar shoes worn by Don Lorenzo Corpi in *Quer pasticciaccio*: 'Le due scarpe [...] priapavano fuori da la vesta che pareveno du affari proibbiti' (QP, 135; His two shoes ... priapated from beneath his garment, like two forbidden objects [AM, 182]).

16 The visual reference is to the official portrait of Giuseppe Garibaldi, which Gadda conveys parodically through echoes of Carducci's *Ode al Piemonte* ('La bionda capellatura dell'eroe'...). On Gadda and Carducci, see Arbasino 1977: 366–7.

17 A recent exploration of the biographical terrain of Gadda's works has uncovered a repressed fratricidal fantasy that could easily account for the displacement of aggression from the Other to the self. See Pedriali 1997.

18 For a discussion of the conflict between Oedipus and Narcissus in Gadda, see Dombroski 1984.

19 'L'infelicità maggiore proveniva dalla povertà della mia famiglia. Per quanto nei primi anni abbiamo avuto delle condizioni abbastanza buone, poi le cose si sono aggravate per errori economici di mio padre. Spendeva più di quanto potesse poi recuperare. Non era un bravo uomo d'affari, sia detto con rispetto.

Era un maniaco della terra, della campagna, della gente brianzola' (Gadda 1993, 156; My greatest unhappiness came from my family's poverty. In the early years our financial situation was sufficiently good, then things got worse on account of my father's economic mistakes. He used to spend more than he could earn. He was not a good business man, let it be said with respect. He was obsessed with the land, the country, the people from Brianza).

20 For an integral Freudian reading of the character of Liliana and of the *Pasticciaccio*, see Amigoni 1995.

21 For a study of sexual imagery in Gadda, see De Benedictis 1991.

22 Cf. *Dejaniera Classis (novella seconda)*, in *Romanzi e Racconti II*: 'ciò non toglie che molti rubino a man salva e le donne abbiano le sottane così corte, che quando son sedute, gli si vedono le cosce, le giarrettiere, le mutandine, fino alla punta di Bellagio, anzi fino alla villa Serbelloni' (1315; this doesn't mean that they are not clever thieves and the women's skirts are so short that when they sit down you can see their thighs, garters, underwear all the way up to Bellagio, actually up to Villa Serbelloni).

4: A Baroque Ethics

1 Manzotti 1996: 208.

2 In the first version of the imaginary dialogue, Gadda had given a more detailed (and delirious) account of why Gonzalo is so belligerent. See Manzotti's comment in reference to lines 205–7 of 'L'Editore chiede venia del recupero' *La cognizione del dolore*, ed. Emilio Manzotti (1987: 490).

3 'Procedere altre non avrebbe solo contraddetto al potente solipsismo che garantisce la vitalità dell'autore: una lucida e cosciente discesa alle Madri avrebbe forse condotto il pellegrino alla suprema rivelazione intellettuale, ormai esente di malizia, che connota i Dante e i Proust [...] E perciò Gadda troverà la salvezza che gli è propria, quel tanto di *purgato animi* che gli compete, in altro che nelle catarsi della pura teoresi, nella contemplazione esaltante dei veri. Per conto suo, lo scatto d'un felice automatismo lo sottrae alla spira dei rimorsi e della disperazione, rettificandola abruptamente in un'umoristica icasticità di rappresentazione [...]': Contini 1963: 10–11.

4 'Non ignoro che in un'accurata descrizione fenomenologica al momento della rappresentazione dovrebbe precedere il momento elegiaco delle nostalgie perdute, espresso in ritmi lunghi, in parole senza senso discorsivo, in viluppi di astratti e in intraducibili sintagmi antropomorfi, spesso intervallati, anzi interotti (il pianto dura, ma il singhiozzo è intermittente), da puntini di sospensione, pausati all'acme del ritmo da punti esclamativi': ibid: 12–13.

5 See Luperini 1981: Vol. 1, 488.

6 Watt 1967: 85–6.

7 See Lorenzini 1995: 324.

8 By making his protagonist object-like, Gadda puts into practice what Angelo Guglielmi has called 'creative realism': a realism without affect and, consequently, devoid of truth claims: 'Nei libri di Gadda non scattano tanto dei giudizi, delle sistemazioni, o dei messaggi quanto e soltanto delle realtà: realtà non moralizzate, che rifiutano ogni intenzione o coloritura ideologica, realtà socialmente non qualificate: realtà esclusivamente fisiche, allo stato neutro' (In Gadda's books it is not so much judgements, theories and messages that spring forth: un-moralized; rather, realities that resist every ideological colouring, realities that are socially without qualification, exclusively physical realities in a neutral state: Guglielmi 1963: 1063).

9 Jameson discusses this process in *Fables of Aggression as* 'the disintegration of the literary exchange, as a socially guaranteed and institutionalized compact between writer and reader' (67).

10 'In itself, the episode of the cat seems harmless enough, just one among Gonzalo's many legendary acts of cruelty. But seen in the light of the re-evocation of his brother's death in the eighth segment of Part Two ("Peccato che uno si fosse buttato in aria, l'aria bonna, a quel modo: ma la gravitazione aveva funzionato" (*CD*, 728)' ['It's a pity that one of them had gone up in the air, the fine air, in that way: but gravity had worked' (*AG*, 204)], the experiment takes on a new meaning, as well as investing the latter passage with jarring sub-textual implications' (Pedriali 1997: 152).

11 'In modern times […] all creative and original speech flows from privation rather than from plenitude: its redoubled energies, far from tapping archaic or undiscovered sources of energy, are proportionate to the massive and well-nigh impenetrable obstacles which aesthetic production must overcome in the age of reification" (Jameson 1979: 81).

5: A Baroque Mystery

1 *Quer pasticciaccio* is not, strictly speaking, an autobiographical novel. Yet, every reader knows that Gadda has assumed the role of the detective in the person of Don Ciccio Ingravallo and that it is the detective's philosophy of entanglement that regulates the narrative. Don Ciccio, moreover, is the host for more than one of Gadda's obsessions, as, for example, when, upon viewing the blackish-red stream of blood that had gushed out of Liliana Balducci's mortal wound, he has Ingravallo recall the Faiti and Cengio mountains, where Gadda's brother Enrico was killed during the war: 'don Ciccio rammemorò subito, con un lontano pianto nell'anima, povera

mamma! [...]' (*QP*, 59). Such an inflection of the authorial self into Don Ciccio does not amount, however, to effacing his distinctiveness as a typically Southern Italian character with whom Gadda feels some deep affinity but who is not Gadda. The same can be said of Commendatore Angeloni, who, like Gadda, is a bachelor living alone, a gourmand, and harbours a certain propensity for young boys, but who retains his physiognomy as a Roman type. These figures are not Gadda; rather, they are absorbed by him and serve the purpose of extending or folding out of his self into the world – another form of baroque excess.

2 Cited in Beverley 1993: 52.

3 Gadda had originally contracted to write for *Letteratura* twelve detective stories which would first be published individually in the journal and then reassembled in a volume for the *Edizioni di Letteratura*. Although nothing ever came of this project, as it was replaced in 1945 by the *Pasticciaccio*, Gadda had already tried his hand at the *giallo* several times before; first with the *Passeggiata autunnale*, then with *Novella seconda* and with a number of stories: 'Un inchino rispettoso,' 'Club delle ombre,' and 'La gazza ladra,' all of which are included in *Accoppiamenti giudiziosi* (*RR II*, 591–920).

4 See Andreini 1988: 140, 145.

5 For the translations from *Quer pasticciaccio* in this chapter, I have used both William Weaver's *AM* and Robert De Lucca's new, as yet unpublished, version of the novel, at times combining and revising slightly both texts.

6 Ferdinando Amigoni has stressed the importance of the number two and its multiples. See Amigoni 1995: 36–40.

7 For a good summary of such a readings, see Dicuonzo 1994: 59–89.

Appendix: Gadda and Fascism

1 Ferrero and Maraini 1968: 18.

2 'Il Gadda non mancherà di allargare il campo della sua esposizione, esaminando quali feconde conseguenze l'impiego dei metalli leggeri sia per avere nell'economia italiana' (*L'Ambrosiano*, 7 September 1931) (Gadda will not be lacking in extending the range of his treatment to examine the fruitful benefits that the deployment of light metals will have for the Italian economy).

3 See also the final article in the series 'I metalli leggeri nel futuro prossimo' (15 September 1931) and another piece written by Arnaldo Mussolini also in reference to the themes discussed by Gadda: 'Metalli leggeri e risorse italiane' (17 September 1931).

4 *L'Ambrosiano*, 13 June 1936.

5 See 'Azoto atmosferico tramutato in pane' (13 April 1937), 'Pane e chimica sintetica' (27 April 1937), 'Automobili e automotrici azionate ad ammoniaca'

(12 May 1937), 'Combustibile italiano' (27 June 1937), 'Le ligniti dell'Appennino e la loro utilizzazione autarchica' (29 September 1939), and 'I problemi della lignite' (10 October 1939).

6 See *QP*, 158–9.

7 *Le Vie d'Italia* 44 (December 1938): 1477–84.

8 See for example 'Divulgazione tecnica: Accessibilità di una rivista,' *L'Ambrosiano*, 12 April 1932, in which, referring to the French review *La science et la vie*, Gadda writes: 'Ameremmo questo esempio imitato in Italia, con eguale serietà e facilità. Condizione prima del successo è quella del suddetto pubblico; è l'esistenza cioè di un ceto di lettori che amino conoscere i dati di fatto, il meccanismo palese o segreto della vita e della tecnica [...] che spogli la sua mente e le sue labbra dalle frasi fatte, dai 'sentito dire', dai nebulosi miti, dai facili entusiasmi e dai facili abbattimenti [...] È giusto ed è necessario che lo spirito dell'uomo moderno si elevi dallo stato mitico, rapsodico ed entusiastico, più proprio degli stregoni, dei dervisci e dei coribanti, a uno stato chiaramente alfabetico e documentario [...]' (We would like to see this example imitated in Italy with the same ease and seriousness. The principal condition for its success is the above-mentioned public: namely, the existence of a class of readers who want to know about the facts behind the manifest or secret mechanism of life and technique.... who divest their minds and their lips of ready-made phrases, of hearsay, of nebulous myths, facile enthusiasm and excitement ... It is right and necessary that the spirit of modern man rise up from the myth, rapture, and enthusiasm typical of witches and magicians to a literate and documentary state ...]

9 'Apologo del Gran Sasso d'Italia,' in *La Gazzetta del Popolo*, 22 November 1934.

10 *Gazzetta del Popolo*, 27 July 1937.

11 *Le vie dell'Italia*, 12 December 1939, 1515.

12 *La Nuova Antologia* 163 (January/February 1941): 283.

13 Ibid 164 (April/May 1941): 392, 395.

14 Ibid: 394–5.

15 See the article 'L'istituto di Studi Romani,' in *Primato delle lettere e delle arti*, 16 August 1942; now in Gadda, *Saggi Giornali Favole I*, ed. Dante Isella (1991: 863–74).

16 'All'insegna dell'alta cultura,' in *Primato delle lettere e delle arti*, 3 February 1943, 54; now in Gadda, *Saggi Giornali Favole I*, ed. Dante Isella (1991: 874–81).

17 On this matter, see Jesi 1968: 108.

18 Pasolini 1963: 64–5.

19 *Eros e Priapo*, in Gadda, *Saggi Giornali Favole II*, ed. Dante Isella (1991: 224, 242). Hereinafter cited in the text as *EP*.

20 The translations here and below are by Arnold and William Hartley.

References

Agosti, Stefano. 1996. 'Quando il linguaggio non va in vacanza: una lettura del Pasticciaccio.' In *Le lingue di Gadda*, ed. Maria Antonietta Terzoli. Rome: Salerno Editore.

Amigoni, Ferdinando. 1995. *La più semplice macchina. Cultura freudiana del 'Pasticciaccio.'* Bologna: Il Mulino.

Andreini, Alba. 1988. 'Codicillo: "Il palazzo degli ori".' In *Studi e testi gaddiani*. Palermo: Sellerio.

Arbasino, Alberto. 1977. *Certi romanzi*. Turin: Einaudi.

Benedetti, Carla. 1997. 'The Enigma of Grief: An Expressionism against the Self.' In *Carlo Emilio Gadda: Contemporary Perspectives*, ed. Manuela Bertone and Robert S. Dombroski. Toronto: University of Toronto Press.

Benjamin, Walter. 1977. *The Origin of German Tragic Drama*. London: New Left.

– 1985. 'Central Park.' *New German Critique* 35 (Winter): 32–58.

Bertone, Manuela. 1993. *Il romanzo come sistema e differenza in C.E. Gadda*. Rome: Editori Riuniti.

– 1977. 'Murderous Desires: Gaddian Matricides from *Novella seconda* to *La cognizione del dolore*.' In *Carlo Emilio Gadda: Contemporary Perspectives*, ed. Manuela Bertone and Robert S. Dombroski. Toronto: University of Toronto Press.

Bertone, Manuela, and Robert S. Dombroski, eds. 1997. *Carlo Emilio Gadda: Contemporary Perspectives*. Toronto: University of Toronto Press.

Beverley, John. 1993. *Against Literature*. Minneapolis and London: University of Minnesota Press.

Biasin, Gian Paolo. 1968. 'L'eros di Gadda e il Priapo di Mussolini.' *Belfagor* 24/4: 473.

Buci-Glucksmann, Christine. 1994. *Baroque Reason. The Aesthetics of Modernity*. Translated by Patrick Camiller. London: Sage.

Calabrese, Omar. 1992. *Neo-Baroque*. Translated by Charles Lambert. Princeton, NJ: Princeton University Press. (Translation of *L'età neobarocca*. Rome and Bari: Laterza, 1987.)

Calvino, Italo. 1988. *Six Memos for the Next Millennium*. Translated by Patrick Creagh. Cambridge, MA: Harvard University Press.

Cases, Cesare. 1958. 'Un ingegnere di letteratura.' In *Mondo operaio* (supplemento scientifico-letterario al n. 5), May.

Contini, Gianfranco. 1963. 'Saggio introduttivo.' In Carlo Emilio Gadda, *La cognizione del dolore*. Turin: Einaudi.

De Benedictis, Maurizio. 1991. *La piega nera. Groviglio stilistico ed enigma della femminilità in C.E. Gadda*. Anzio: De Rubeis Editore.

Deleuze, Gilles. 1988. *Le pli. Leibniz et le Baroque*. Paris: Le Editions de Minuit.

– 1993. *The Fold: Leibniz and the Baroque*. Translated by Tom Conley. Minneapolis: University of Minnesota Press.

Dicuonzo, Angelo R. 1994. 'La coscienza della complessità. Sulla struttura del "Pasticciaccio" gaddiano.' In *Lingua e stile* 29/1: 59–89.

Dombroski, Robert S. 1984a. *L'esistenza ubbidiente. Letteratura e fascismo*. Naples: Guida Editore.

– 1984b. 'Overcoming Oedipus: Self and Society in *La cognizione del dolore*.' *MLN*, Italian Issue, 99/1 (January): 123–43.

– 1994. *Properties of Writing: Ideological Discourse in Modern Italian Fiction*. Baltimore: Johns Hopkins University Press.

Ferrero, Ernesto, and Dacia Maraini. 1968. 'C.E. Gadda: come scrittore, come uomo.' *Prisma* 5: 14–19.

Fido, Franco, Rena A. Syska-Lamparska, and Pamela D. Stewart, eds. 1998. *Studies for Dante: Essays in Honor of Dante Della Terza*. Florence: Edizioni Cadmo.

Freud, Sigmund. 1989. *The Freud Reader*, ed. Peter Gay. New York: Norton.

Gadda, Carlo Emilio. 1963. *La cognizione del dolore*. Turin: Einaudi.

– 1969. *Acquainted with Grief*. Translated by William Weaver. New York: George Braziller.

– 1985. *That Awful Mess on Via Merulana*. Translated by William Weaver. London: Quartet Books.

– 1987. *La cognizione del dolore*. Edited by Emilio Manzotti. Turin: Einaudi.

– 1988, 1989, 1991, 1992, 1993b. *Opere di Carlo Emilio Gadda*. General editor Dante Isella. Milan: Garzanti. (The editing of the individual volumes was carried out by a team assembled by Dante Isella, which included, in addition to Isella, Raffaella Rodondi, Guido Lucchini, Emilio Manzotti, Giorgio Pinotti, Liliana Orlando, Clelia Martignoni, Claudio Vela, Gianmarco Gasperi, Ranco Gavazzeni, Maria Antonietta Terzoli, Andrea Silvestri, and Paola Italia.)

– 1993a. 'Per favore mi lasci nell'ombra.' In *Interviste 1950–1972*, ed. Claudio Vela. Milan: Adelphi.

Guglielmi, Angelo. 1963. 'Carlo Emilio Gadda.' In *Letteratura Italiana. I Contemporanei*, 2 vols. Milan: Marzorati.

Hainsworth, Peter. 1997. 'Fascism and Anti-Fascism in Gadda.' In *Carlo Emilio Gadda. Contemporary Perspectives*, ed. Manuela Bertone and Robert S. Dombroski. Toronto: University of Toronto Press.

Jameson, Federic. 1979. *Fables of Agression: Wyndham Lewis: the Modernist as Fascist*. Berkeley: University of California Press.

Jencks, Charles. 1995. *The Architecture of the Jumping Universe*. New York: St Martin's.

Jesi, Fulvio. 1968. *La cultura di destra*. Turin: Einaudi.

Kristeva, Julia. 1989. *Black Sun*. New York: Columbia University Press.

Layzer, David. 1990. *Cosmogenesis. The Growth of Order in the Universe*. New York: Oxford University Press.

Lipparini, Micaela. 1984. *Le metafore del vero. Percezione e deformazione figurativa in Carlo Emilio Gadda*. Pisa: Pacini.

Lorenzini, Niva. 1995. 'Gadda, il mito, la "deformazione".' In *Mito e esperienze letterarie*, ed. Fausto Curi and Niva Lorenzini. Bologna: Pendragon.

Lucchini, Guido. 1997. 'Gadda's Freud.' In *Carlo Emilio Gadda: Contemporary Perspectives*, ed. Manuela Bertone and Robert S. Dombroski. Toronto: University of Toronto Press.

Luperini, Romano. 1981. *Il Novecento*, 2 vols. Turin: Loescher.

Manacorda, Giuliano. 1967. *Storia della letteratura italiana contemporanea*. Rome: Editori Riuniti.

Manganaro Jean-Paul. 1994. *Le Baroque et l'Ingénieur. Essai sur l'écriture de Carlo Emilio Gadda*. Paris: Seuil.

Manzoni, Alessandro. 1966. *I promessi sposi*. Edited by Lanfranco Caretti. Milan: Mursia.

– 1972. *The Betrothed*. Translated by Bruce Penman. Harmondsworth: Penguin.

Manzotti, Emilio. 1996. '*La cognizione del dolore* di Carlo Emilio Gadda.' In *Letteratura italiana. Le Opere*, IV/2. *Il Novecento. La ricerca letteraria*. Turin: Einaudi.

Manzotti, Emilio, ed. 1987. *La cognizione del dolore*. Turin: Einaudi.

Maravall, José Antonio. 1986, *Culture of the Baroque. Analysis of a Historical Structure*. Minneapolis. University of Minnesota Press.

Martinetti, Piero. 1904. *Introduzione alla metafisica*. Turin: Einaudi.

Mazzotta, Giuseppe. 1989. 'Manzoni e il barocco: La biblioteca di Don Ferrante.' In *Perspectives on Nineteenth-Century Italian Novels*, ed. Guido Pugliese. Toronto: Dovehouse Editions, 1989.

Miller, D.A. 1988. *The Novel and the Police*. Berkeley and Los Angeles: University of California Press.

Pasolini, Pier Paolo. 1963. 'Un passo di Gadda.' *L'Europa Letteraria* 4/20–1: 61–7.

Pedriali, Federica. 1997. 'The Mark of Cain: Morning and Dissimulation in the Works of Carlo Emilio Gadda.' In *Carlo Emilio Gadda: Contemporary Perspectives*, ed. Manuela Bertone and Robert S. Dombroski. Toronto: University of Toronto Press.

Raimondi, Ezio. 1990. *Barocco moderno: Carlo Emilio Gadda e Roberto Longhi*. Bologna: CUSL.

Roscioni, Gian Carlo. 1969. *La disarmonia prestabilita*. Turin: Einaudi.

Roscioni, Gian Carlo, ed. 1974. *Meditazione milanese*. Turin: Einaudi.

Sbragia, Albert. 1996. *Carlo Emilio Gadda and the Modern Macaronic*. Gainesville: University of Florida Press.

Seroni, Adriano. 1969. *Gadda*, Florence: La Nuova Italia.

Sokel, Walter. 1959. *The Writer in Extremis*. Stanford, CA: Stanford University Press.

Turner, Bryan S. 1994. Introduction to Christine Buci-Glucksmann's *Baroque Reason. The Aesthetics of Modernity*. London: Sage.

Watt, Ian. 1967. *The Rise of the Novel*. Berkeley and Los Angeles: University of California Press.

Index

Agosti, Stefano, 55
Alfieri, Vittorio, 137n
Amigoni, Ferdinando, 102, 139n, 141n, 143n
Andreini, Alba, 143n
Arbasino, Alberto, 140n

Bakhtin, Mikhail, 97
Baudelaire, Charles, 34
Belli, Giuseppe Gioachino, 111, 114
Benedetti, Carla, 76, 81, 89
Benjamin, Walter, 30, 35–7
Bergson, Henrì, 45, 47, 49–50
Bertone, Manuela, 82, 135n
Beverley, John, 5, 136n, 143n
Biasin, Gian Paolo, 117
Böcklin, Arnold, 51, 139n
Broch, Hermann, 135n
Buci-Glucksmann, Christine, 25, 32, 34–5, 135n
Buonarotti, Michelangelo, 71

Calabrese, Omar, 136n, 137n
Calderon della Barca, Pedro, 35
Calvino, Italo, 11, 96, 136n, 137n
Carducci, Giosué, 15, 51, 140n
Caretti, Lanfranco, 140n

Cases, Cesare, 119
Céline, Louis Ferdinand, 71, 135n
Ciano, Edda, 109
Contini, Gianfranco, 6, 55, 80–2, 141n
Croce, Benedetto, 4, 138n

D'Annunzio, Gabriele, 5, 43
Dante Alighieri, 32, 74, 80–1
De Benedictis, Maurizio, 141n
De Bono, Emilio, 122, 127
De Chirico, Giorgio, 18, 61–51, 139n, 140n
Defoe, Daniel, 88
Della Terza, Dante, x
Deleuze, Gilles, 6–8, 10, 18, 72, 84, 104, 107, 110, 137n
De Lucca, Robert, x, 143n
Dicuonzo, Angelo, 143n
d'Ors, Eugenio, 4
Dossi, Carlo, 55

Faldella, Giovanni, 55
Ferrero, Ernesto, 143n
Fido, Franco, x
Folengo, Teofilo, 92
Foscolo, Ugo, 51

Freud, Sigmund, 72, 79, 88–9

Garibaldi, Giuseppe, 140n
Gentile, Giovanni, 138n
Gracian y Morales, Baldasar, 92
Gruppo 63, 48
Guglielmi, Angelo, 142n

Hainsworth, Peter, 118, 129
Hartley, Arnold, 144n
Hartley, William, 144n
Heidegger, Martin, 43

Isella, Dante, 135n, 135n, 137n, 138n,
    139n, 140n, 144n

Jameson, Fredric, 19, 54, 64, 92, 110,
    140n, 142n
Jenks, Charles, ix, 135n
Jesi, Furio, 144n
Joyce, James, 55, 74, 135n

Kant, Imanuel, 44
Kristeva, Julia, 76–7

Lacan, Jacques, 67–70, 72, 129
Layzer, David, 135n
Leibniz, Gottfried Wilhelm, 6–7, 45,
    72, 136n
Leopardi, Giacomo, 15
Lewis, Wyndham, 54–5, 92, 110

Lipparini, Micaela, 140n
Lorenzini, Niva, 88, 142n
Lucchini, Guido, 49, 130, 137n
Luperini, Romano, 86–7, 142n
Lukacs, Georg, 7

Macchiavelli, Niccolò, 36
Manacorda, Giuliano, 117

Manganaro, Jean Paul, 135n
Manzoni, Alessandro, 11–12, 21–2, 32,
    53, 136n, 140n

Manzotti, Emilio, 74, 79, 86, 136n,
    137n, 140n, 141n
Maraini, Dacia, 117, 143n
Maravall, José Antonio, 135n
Martinetti, Piero, 44, 138n, 139n
Mazzotta, Giuseppe, 136n
Miller, D.A., 101
Munch, Edward, 19
Musil, Robert, 135n
Mussolini, Arnaldo, 120, 143n
Mussolini, Benito, 11, 107–8, 115, 117,
    123–6, 130–2

Nietzsche, Friedrich, 130

Pasolinji, Pier Paolo, 90–2, 129
Pedriali, Federica, 83, 140n
Penman, Bruce, 140n
Pirandello, Luigi, 43, 49
Porta, Carlo, 114
Proust, Marcel, 81, 135n

Quevedo, y Villegas, Francisco
    Gomez de, 31

Rabelais, François, 92
Raimondi, Ezio, 135n
Rodondi, Raffaella, 137n
Roscioni, Gian Carlo, 44, 86, 139n

Saussure, Ferdinand de, 139n
Sbragia, Albert, 135n
Schopenhauer, Arthur, 136n
Seroni, Adriano, 117

Shakespeare, William, 35

Sokel, Walter, 138n

Sterne, Lawrence, 55

Stewart, Pamela D., x

Svevo, Italo, 43, 137n

Swift, Jonathan, 55

Syska-Lamparska, Rena A., x

Turner, Bryan S., 135n

Verga, Giovanni, 53

Watt, Ian, 87

Weaver, William, x, 70, 136n, 137n, 143n